GRIDIRON WISDOM

A PLAYBOOK FOR LEADERSHIP

Ron McIntyre

Enjoy the Read!

Ron

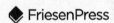 FriesenPress

One Printers Way
Altona, MB R0G 0B0
Canada

www.friesenpress.com

ISBN
978-1-03-830086-7 (Hardcover)
978-1-03-830085-0 (Paperback)
978-1-03-830087-4 (eBook)

1. SPORTS & RECREATION, FOOTBALL

Distributed to the trade by The Ingram Book Company

Using the term "Eskimo" in the team name is a historical reflection and does not imply endorsement or appropriation of indigenous culture. We acknowledge the sensitivity of language and aim to use it respectfully and in accordance with contemporary standards. We intend to honour the legacy of the name while promoting inclusivity and cultural awareness.

I offer this book as a tribute to the unsung heroes behind the scenes—the volunteers who serve as coaches, trainers, and managers. Their selfless commitment fuels the spirit of the game and shapes champions on and off the field.

TABLE OF CONTENTS

FOREWORD BY
JOHN SHORT

In many circumstances, it is reasonable to expect any publication of a football team's "history" to provide a play-by-play, year-by-year, tackle-after-tackle account of all that has affected an organization from Year One to the present.

Writer Ron McIntyre, to his credit, has followed another route. This rendition of history reflects one man's love for a game that first touched him during childhood and continues to shape his existence at 64 years of age, well into retirement from years as a player, teacher and coach.

"Looking back, my first memory of football was how much fun it was to play," McIntyre said during a relaxed interview, one of the countless discussions he arranged and conducted before sitting down for the first of many hours at his computer. "One of the first things I learned in high school was that in addition to fun, you need discipline to play the game well."

At about the same time, this teenage budding linebacker recognized that teamwork and commitment were excellent ways to bond with on-field allies and, ultimately, build several lasting friendships. "As a player, you have things in common with other players in the sport, not just guys on your team."

Veteran coach John Belmont, included in the book as one of many whose mentorship became valuable to the author, said recently he was not surprised that McIntyre grew big enough "and tough enough" to play four years as a starter at York University in Toronto.

"Even in high school, it was obvious that he liked the contact of his position," said Belmont. "Ron was a good tackler and would never give up on a play. He was willing to hit anybody at any time."

McIntyre quickly found coaching a particular interest and praised Frank Cosentino, his York head coach and a former CFL starter at quarterback, for encouraging him. "He made a big difference in my attitude. "When I started to play, I was probably motivated by anger. As the competition got tougher, I learned that it was more important to be smart."

That lesson, absorbed through four years of Cosentino's positive leadership on what was consistently a 0.500-level team, clearly remains a vital influence. If proof is necessary, consider that McIntyre spent about 35 years as a head or assistant coach in Alberta high schools, many of them in close communication with the late Jim Gilfillan, who is still recognized as a legend among the long list of accomplished teachers of football, complete with citizenship and sportsmanship, to young athletes in the province's lengthy football history.

This commitment to football and young athletes was consistently broadened when Peter Connellan at the University of Calgary and Gary DeMan of Calgary's St. Francis High School were readily available for advice and guidance. "All of these men, and many others, made it clear that lessons learned from football can be helpful later in life," says McIntyre. "One of the best things they did was show me and others a template for programs that were successful in many ways."

McIntyre spoke comfortably about what he hopes and expects this book to foster: "A positive approach to coaching the game." This broad-spectrum analysis includes a return to competitive school sports to the level it once held in most educational institutions. "The emphasis on healthy competition has diminished in recent years and there is a fear that important lessons and mentorship could be lost without these experiences. If we wait much longer, it is almost certain that the decline in the value of sports for students will continue. The best time to tackle the issue is right now.

INTRODUCTION

Edmonton had a lot of kids in the 1960s and 1970s who spent their summers on their relatives' farms on the prairies. My country refuge was in Wynyard, Saskatchewan, where my mother's family farmed two miles south of town. Summers were a lot of fun for a city boy, as my cousins Scott and Shannon were too young to handle machinery, so life was easy and free. We were roughly the same age and soon to enter adolescence, so we took great delight in enjoying the outdoors and eating six times a day, as was the custom. Returning to Edmonton was never easy, as Wynyard felt like home.

The drive to Edmonton took close to eight hours, and the trip home when I entered my grade seven year felt a touch different, as my mom's younger sister accompanied us. As our Chrysler Saratoga packed with three adults and my sister made the final turn toward our home in Greenfields, I remember rolling down the window and waving to my buddies, telling them to meet me in a few minutes at Vernon Barford Jr. High to play football.

My life quickly changed, however, and events unfolded in slow motion as my mother met me in the bedroom and informed me that things were about to change. Dad was unhappy and would no longer be living with us. The intensity of my reaction was on a scale that I have not felt since that late-August day. My sister (Lori) and I could make little sense of the complexity of adult relationships. I remember my aunt retreating to the front doorstep, hanging her head, and sharing our grief.

Within minutes, my friends bounced up to my back door with a football and proclaimed it was time to play. "Hurry up!" they yelled.

My mind and body were no longer connected, and I tried to find an excuse to stay home, but my dad insisted I join them.

I was having a hard time that day, and someone asked if I was okay. I replied that I had some bad news and told them a lie about a change in my mother's work status. My friends understood that my mother had a great job in the airline industry that gave us free airfare around the world and that to lose those benefits would be sad. In truth, I felt an overwhelming sense of sadness and shame.

In complete chaos where nothing made sense, a pickup game of football attempted to ground me. I could not shake off what had just happened; I was wounded. The rules and structure of the game made more sense that day than the events that shook my family to its core.

Pickup football that summer evolved to bantam football in the fall. The coaching and mentoring I received through the game continued for another decade. Football made sense to me, and it still does—the rules and the aim to win are simple and noble. Finding order in the chaos of adolescence can come from different places. Still, football was the game that introduced me to people and friends who pointed me to a happier future if I played by the rules. I know now that I was not alone in needing the structure that football provided. It was a difficult road to adulthood, but I had a lot of help and remained connected to the game in adulthood through coaching and teaching social studies.

For thirty-five years I was occasionally humbled by young people with exemplary writing skills. I knew they were good, but I only knew how good once I stopped marking papers and started writing. I have come to appreciate what I have put thousands of students through. The last year of my life would have been much easier if I had paid more attention to my humanities teachers.

I have one published work which found its way to the last chapter of a book titled *The Complexities of Authority in the Classroom*. It is unlikely to appear on the *New York Times* Best Seller list, but hopefully someone, somewhere will read it. A little positive feedback would be welcome. Writing was and is more challenging than motivating a team to practise a tackling drill.

People who know a thing or two about writing say you should focus on topics you understand. Having spent forty years connected to the game, I am far from humble on anything related to football, particularly coaching. I organized this book around themes that became apparent as the interviews progressed. Originally, I intended to highlight the teams chronologically, but a different approach was taken. For those who like a straight-line approach to history, I will use that style to shed some light on how I've come to appreciate the game and its best teams.

It was in the late 1950s when the die was cast regarding my future love affair with football. Upon seeing me as a newborn, my Grandpa McIntyre remarked, "He's going to be a football player. Look at the size of his hands!" *Little* did Grandpa Mac know that my DNA was overloaded with slow-twitch muscle fibres that developed long ago in Scandinavia and the Scottish Highlands near Oban.

Early in life, I knew my dad was part of Wynyard, Saskatchewan's football folklore. His nickname was "Moose"; I always hoped it referenced his physicality and determination and not his intellect as the fullback on the team that won the provincial six-man championship. Although I never met the man, Scotty Martin was his QB. My dad's memories of his leadership were and remain special to him. Dad's admiration for his teammates and their accomplishments gave me a glimpse into what sports had to offer. I was proud of his accomplishments on the field and off.

My first football as a youngster looked more like a rugby ball than the ball we have today. I played catch with any adult who could wrap their hands around that blimp. I can still see that ball with its three laces hanging on for dear life. It was easy to catch, owing to its size, though it was not much of a ball. But it was mine.

Elementary school passed, and grade seven was the chance to play organized football. It was a tough initiation to football, and the violence inflicted on us tykes by coaches trying to get us over our fear of contact was never again matched. Fifty years later, the tackling drills we were forced to do still send chills down my teammates' spines at reunions. We had good teams despite ourselves and represented southwest Edmonton with pride.

In late October 1973, with a temperature of -10°C, the Southwest Edmonton Vikings ran onto the frozen tundra of Kinsmen Park to play their hated rivals, the west-end Raiders, for the city championship. It was cold and to make it even worse, I had to sit in the sauna for a couple of hours before the game to make sure I made the weight limit of 160 pounds, which was the standard for bantam football in Edmonton. I made the weigh-in and immediately devoured some sandwiches before the "football on ice" game.

Upon arrival at Kinsmen Park, we were relieved that the city of Edmonton had graded the field and exposed the rock-hard ground for us. The layers and layers of clothes we wore that day were little help for our exposed skin and feet. Today, Child Services would have stopped the proceedings and arrested the coaches. Today's bantam players have the luxury of playing on cushioned artificial fields with sideline heaters—they have no idea.

That city final happened almost fifty years ago and was a big deal for us kids. We were not pleased about the weather, but we still played to win. Unfortunately, we lost that game, but none of us had limbs amputated due to frostbite. Players on both sides ricocheted off that frozen ground like rubber balls, but there was no place we would rather have been that day.

I cannot forget how much that game meant to us young fellows. Our fullback and best player, Glen Irvin, was throwing up in the bathroom before the game. Many of the names from that team have evaporated, but Irvin will not be forgotten. When the time came, we buckled up our chinstraps, climbed over a snowbank, and entered the fray. The names and faces have faded, but we were brothers under siege that day.

My unremarkable career as a player continued through high school and on to the college ranks. The Scona Lords exposed my adolescent brain to the world's reality, as my coaches were exceptional men. I owe them an apology for my stupidity. Upon graduation, I found a school a couple of thousand miles away that would accept me. I ran into another great group of coaches led by my boyhood idol and former Eskimo, Frank Cosentino.

Cosentino once chased us kids off the rink in Edmonton as we were not allowed to be there with hockey sticks during family skating time. He was a two-time national championship coach at Western University in Ontario, and York was lucky to have him. He made a significant impression on us.

My teammates at York reminded me daily that I was an Albertan. On day three of my first training camp, my nickname became "Cowboy," and I did my best to live up to it. For most of my teammates, I was the first Albertan they had ever met. They had little time for my ranting about how everything was bigger and better in the West.

After waking up on draft day in disbelief that all those CFL teams had overlooked me, I was not done with football. Since playing was out, coaching was the thing to do. In my first year of coaching, the McNally Tigers junior team went winless, and as their defensive coordinator, we may have set records for most points allowed, but I don't think I'll check the archives to verify that. What is peculiar about that first year is that I enjoyed it despite our record.

At about the same time, I met my dream girl, Michele Kmech. She ticked off all the essential boxes. She was smart, loved kids, and was a brunette. She also had a weakness for football. Both of her brothers, Dean and Jay, played, as did her father. He was an undersized guard and all-star with the 1950s Eskimos. Between her IQ and her athletic pedigree, I was positive the DNA of my children would get an upgrade from her side. I was correct, as my son and daughter, Michael and Allyson, have outdone their old man.

The tide turned quickly at McNally in the late 1980s, and we had a good run. We had some excellent mentor coaches who brought out the best in the players and us young coaches. Jim Gilfillan, Alex Beekman, Larry Dufresne, and Gerald Kunyk were great coaches, and we won several championships. McNally was a smaller school, but our athletes were talented and the school's administration was committed to success.

After stints coaching at several high schools, the University of Alberta, and for the Edmonton Huskies, I often wondered how we compared to our American neighbours. After learning about Alberta's best coaches, I am confident our most talented coaches would succeed anywhere.

Playing the game properly means more than winning championships or generating lots of money. The teams in this book made people richer but not as usually defined. In many of the conversations I conducted for this book, there would be a pause and the person being interviewed would quietly say one of two things: "The game changed my life," or, "I don't know where I'd be if it weren't for football." None of the people I interviewed got rich playing football, but they felt blessed through the coaching/playing experience.

The leaders in this book left no stone unturned in trying to be better coaches. They were honest with themselves and their teams. For some, their faith was the foundation; for others, it was respect for human dignity. Whatever the reason, they won on and off the field. But they didn't do it alone. Coaches must have an eye for talent, including finding sympathetic and supportive spouses. Marriage is the ultimate team game, and all coaches understand that truth. The men interviewed for this book mentioned the necessity of teamwork in their marriages. Without their spouses' support, their work would not have been possible.

Teammates, like spouses, depend on each other for success. The sport does not matter; you need the other person if it involves two or more teammates. The word "need" in football is crucial, as everyone's safety is at stake. A missed block, lack of communication, errant pass, or misplay can result in serious injury. As one coach told us, "You have to have each other's backs, so we don't get our backs broken."

As an old guy who spent fifty years as a player, fan, and coach, I understand the attraction of football. Sports of all shapes and sizes have always intrigued me. Besides, football, hockey, baseball, and basketball are important excuses not to finish everything on my wife's to-do list. Hockey in the winter and spring, baseball in the summer, and football in the fall keep me from being the handyman my male ancestors were.

Hockey's physicality does not take a back seat to football, but it is so fast that the tactics are difficult to figure out. Fighting has no place in any other sport, yet I understand why we enjoy the odd brawl on the ice. Football's violence is controlled and understandable—hockey's, not so much.

Baseball is America's favourite pastime but not its favourite sport. You need something to do in the summer while you wait for the leaves and crops to ripen, so even here in Canada we turn on baseball. Baseball provides excellent drama, but swinging sticks at a ball does not satisfy our thirst for contact between big and fast people. One-hundred-mile-an-hour fastballs on the inside of the plate help enforce baseball's code of conduct but do not match the physicality that football provides.

The athleticism required to play basketball is undeniable. How can freakishly tall men throw down three-pointers, control the ball on the dribble, and make no-look passes to their teammates? The problem with basketball is that it is hard to relate to people who duck to get under doorways.

At the very least, sports provide enjoyment and fitness for the participants. At their best, sports improve the individual's team skills, self-discipline, and self-knowledge. Football teams in Alberta's past and present have managed a few times to get it almost entirely correct, so let us introduce them and later look at the paths they took to succeed. The teams that captured my imagination and the imaginations of many Albertans were the Edmonton Eskimos of the 1950s, Edmonton Huskies of the 1960s, Raymond Comets, St. Francis Browns of Calgary, and the University of Calgary Dinos of the 1980s. These were legendary teams on the field and had a lasting impact on our province.

Other teams have won more games, like the Wetaskiwin teams led by Norm Brown or the LCI teams of Lethbridge led by Jim Whitelaw. Brown's record of 46–0–3 is remarkable for any team in any sport. It was claimed to be the North American record at the time. I hope their fantastic story unfolds and is soon known outside the community of Wetaskiwin, where Coach Brown had the local field named after him. The five-in-a-row Eskimos of the late 1970s and early 1980s were other teams that warranted attention but for different reasons. Their dominance of the CFL was unprecedented and has yet to be matched. The teams I chose to feature in this book differed because they dominated at provincial and national levels while making a lasting mark on their communities.

I want to thank the dozens of men and women who shared their football and life experiences. Asking someone you do not know to bare their soul about their life's work is risky, but thankfully they agreed and my curiosity was rewarded.

The book revolves around the following gentlemen, followed by the people who provided additional background.

- Peter Connellan, former University of Alberta hockey player. Coached high school and Dinos football. Educator.
- Liz Connellan, former University of Alberta curler (Western Canadian champion) and provincial representative in women's curling. Educator.
- Tony Fasano, former Stamford High School (Niagara Falls) and McMaster University player. Coached peewee, bantam, high school, and university football (USA/Canada). Businessman.
- Luigi Fortini, former player at St. Francis High School. Current principal of St. Francis.
- Tom Higgins, former Colonia High School (New Jersey), South Carolina State, and NFL/CFL player. Coached university and professional levels.
- Keith Holliday, former Viscount Bennett High School and University of Calgary player. Firefighter.
- Rick Medcke, former Edmonton Huskie and University of Alberta player. Coached peewee, bantam, high school, junior, and university football. Businessman.
- Jack Neumann, former sports information director at the University of Calgary.

- Mike Newans, former equipment manager and "spiritual leader" of the 1980s Dinos.
- George Paleniuk, former Victoria High School, Edmonton Wildcat, and University of Manitoba/Alberta player. Coached peewee, bantam, high school, junior, and university football. Professional scout and businessman.
- Tony Spoletini, former St. Francis High School, University of Calgary, and CFL player. Businessman.
- Gary DeMan, former St. Mary's High School and Calgary Junior player. Coached St. Francis High School and junior football. Educator.
- Sally DeMan, former University of Alberta basketball player. Educator.
- Tom Forzani, former St. Francis High School, Utah State, and CFL player. Coached high school, junior, university, and professional football. Businessman.
- Chris Lewis, former St. Francis High School, University of Calgary, and CFL player. Coached peewee, bantam, high school, and university football. Businessman.
- Brian Dudley, created a league for football in southwestern Alberta. Coached Raymond High School and junior high school football.
- Blair Bennett, former Bonnie Doon player. Businessman.
- Marc Bennett, former Salisbury High School and University of Alberta player. Businessman.
- Bob Gibb, coached high school football. Educator.
- Bernie Orr, played and coached at Raymond High School.
- Jim Ralph, played at Raymond High School. Coached high school football. School board member.
- Jack Schwartzberg, former Victoria High School, University of Alberta, and CFL player. Businessman.
- Pop Ivy, the only person to coach in the Canadian professional league, the National Football League, and the American Football League. An all-American at the University of

Oklahoma, he coached with Bud Wilkinson for six years before coming to Edmonton.

- John Belmont, former Ross Sheppard High School player. Manager of the Arizona State baseball team. Coached bantam, high school, university, and professional levels. Educator and businessman.
- Brian Dickinson, former Edmonton Wildcat. Coached high school, junior, university, and professional levels. Businessman.
- Jim Gilfillan, former player at Victoria High School. Coached high school and junior levels. Educator.
- Mike Kmech, former Edmonton Huskie and Edmonton Eskimo. Coached bantam and junior football. Businessman.
- Bo Jereniuk, former Victoria High School and Edmonton Wildcat player. Coached at high school and junior levels. Educator.
- Dr. Garry Smith, former Bonnie Doon High School and University of Alberta player. Coached at the university level. Educator.
- Dennis Kadatz, former Strathcona High School and Edmonton Huskies player. Junior and university coach. Athletic director.
- Denise Kadatz, educator.
- Mike Eurchuk, former Strathcona High School and University of Alberta player. Coached high school and managed the Edmonton Huskies. Businessman.
- Warren Hansen, former player with the Edmonton Huskies. Coached junior football. Businessman.
- Hugh McColl Jr., former Strathcona High School Junior and university player. Businessman.
- Marv Roberts, former Ponoka High player and equipment manager with the Edmonton Huskies. Businessman.
- Jack Rutherford, former Edmonton Wildcats player. General manager of the Edmonton Wildcats. Businessman.

- George Spanach, former Ross Sheppard High School, Edmonton Huskies, and professional player. Coached at junior and university levels. Businessman.
- Cam Stewart, former Strathcona High School player. Businessman.

The following people either led me to this project or were of great help in helping me complete it.

- Frank Cosentino, former CFL QB and Canadian university coach. Canadian sports historian and professor. Coach Cosentino wrote seventeen books on sports in Canada.
- Jim Gilfillan, a fellow coach and educator, was a great friend for forty-five years until his passing in 2018. Jim's contributions to the lives of his fellow coaches and players were well known in Edmonton.
- Dr. Rod Macleod, professor emeritus at the University of Alberta. His contributions to documenting and preserving Western Canadian history are exemplary.
- Mike Kmech, my father-in-law. He passed away in 2022 and answered thousands of questions about those Eskimos teams. His experience as a guard on the 1950s and early 1960s Eskimos teams was invaluable for me as a young coach.
- John Short's encouragement and insights were invaluable as a former editor and writer with the Canadian Press, the *Edmonton Journal,* and the *Edmonton Sun* newspapers. John also served as the director of public relations with the Edmonton Oilers.
- Tony Spoletini made this book possible. Getting Tony to fork over Dinos secrets and contact numbers wasn't too difficult after I spent nearly a month's worth of teacher's pension on Spolumbo's sausage!
- Tom Wilkinson, a former CFL player and University of Alberta head coach, and a member of the CFL and the University of Wyoming halls of fame. Tom's insights into player leadership and successful teams were invaluable.

-1-

WIN, WIN, WIN!

Football dressing rooms before games are difficult to forget. They are repugnant. The rancid odour of equipment and the smells emanating from sewers overwhelmed by endless flushing leaves one wishing for a westerly wind. Who could forget the nervous eyes darting around the room? Those same eyes betray the fight-or-flight instinct that rages within the combatants. Add to that the tearing sound of athletic tape and gasps from players as ankles, shoulders, and knees get last-minute attention from frantic trainers and coaches. Closer to game time, the tension turns to expectation with courageous voices rallying their teammates and the clacking of plastic cleats on pavement moving toward the exit. The queasy mix of "goings on" pulls the participants onto a stage where the fear of losing may be equal to or greater than the glory associated with victory.

The locker room before championship games is electric. In 1966, three dozen boys from Victoria High School anxiously awaited their chance to leave their locker room to show the world the champions of Edmonton. They anticipated calming or encouraging words from their coach, but instead the pregame speech turned out to be the sounds of the head coach hurling the contents of his stomach into one of the two toilets in the Clarke Stadium locker room.

Yet, here he was in Edmonton, immersed in a high school football game. A captain demanded of his teammates that under no condition should their coach, Mr. Bob Dean, care more about winning the championship than they did. Bo Jereniuk, the star Redmen QB, recalled over fifty years later the scene in which the normally composed and carefully orchestrated pregame broke into chaos. The players literally fought each other to get out of the locker room. Everyone struggled to be the first to deliver the knockout blow to the Blue Devils of Eastglen High School. As the last of his players left the locker room, Coach Dean emerged from the stall and confidently said to his QB, "Bo . . . I think we're already up a TD."

Bob Dean was no stranger to high-pressure situations. He had played in several college bowl games, kicked the game-winning convert in the 1954 Grey Cup, and served in the Korean War. Dean described his two years in the Korean War as "experiences I wouldn't sell for a million dollars and wouldn't buy for a penny." He didn't see himself as a "go get 'em guy," but he was proud of his two years of service in the United States Army.

The defence of South Korea against China and North Korea was going poorly until General MacArthur and his staff devised a plan to land an army at the rear of the invading force in the city of Inchon. The plan was brilliantly carried out on September 15, 1950. It threatened the enemy's supply lines and their retreat back to the north. Bob Dean was deployed to Inchon and saw his first action there.

Dean recalls a stretch of road that the soldiers called the "Indianapolis Speedway," as it was one hundred yards long and connected two units of United Nations Forces. The main line of resistance separated the United Nations and the communists. The Speedway was vulnerable to Chinese snipers, so the Americans would usually travel the road at night and get up a full head of steam to get across the opening quickly. The crossing was very dangerous, and few volunteered to do it.

One day Dean's friend, Red Henry from Idaho, said to Dean, "Let's make a buck doing this job." Dean recalled, "If the Chinese sniper got lucky, your parents got ten thousand dollars and a letter saying how sorry they were that you had lost a son. But if there was evidence you got shot at, you got extra pay. When we finished the run, Henry said, 'Let's put a bullet through the windshield and in the backseat and make some extra pay.' It sounded good to me. We did it, and we got extra pay!" A week later, a mechanic contacted the two and said he couldn't find any evidence of the bullet. Dean was impressed when his friend quickly replied that he had dug the bullet out of the seat and sent it home as a souvenir. Henry saved the two storytellers a stint in the stockade.

The Vic team that Dean led to consecutive championships in 1965 and 1966 reflected Dean's background. His upbringing was in a working-class neighbourhood in "Steeltown," Pittsburgh, Pennsylvania, where his parents tolerated football but insisted on strict classical music training for their son. The Korean War interrupted football at the University of Maryland and later with the Eskimos. Dean understood discipline early on through his caring parents, and it followed him through the military and football. Still, he found time to have a lifetime of fun and near misses. His students were lucky to have a human who understood the complexities of being young and how discipline was needed to save them from themselves.

The Eskimos (now known as the Elks), the Raymond Comets, the University of Calgary Dinos, and the Edmonton Huskies of the early 1960s and the St. Francis Browns had formulas for success that deserve everyone's attention. Other teams in Alberta's rich football history have had long-term success, and some have even had better winning records than the teams in this book. Still, few have captured the imagination of Alberta's football community like these five teams.

For some, football is a violent, unimaginative game played by massive people driven by animal instincts. In many ways, they are correct; it is a demanding sport played in sometimes harsh conditions (especially in Alberta) by humans who compete to win. Critics of the game say its brutality does not belong in modern society. Rare are those players who wish they had never played.

Strangers to the game do not get to see the beautiful interactions between young men and their mentors who enthusiastically share their time and experiences. This book spends most of its time exploring the values and techniques that Alberta's best football coaches used to achieve their goals and improve their communities.

Coaches know that a game's outcome is in the players' hands, and the calls and decisions they make during a game do not matter if the players aren't prepared to tackle, block, and execute the plays properly. Although the players ultimately control the outcome, the coaches' values matter greatly. The intensity and physicality of football leave the players desperate for advice on how to cope. This is where optimistic, disciplined leadership teaches life skills as well.

Principles such as sacrifice, fulfilling your potential, caring more for your team's success than personal glory, and respecting opponents are commonplace in successful locker rooms. To bring dozens of individuals together and agree on hard-to-reach values is a massive challenge. The behind-the-scenes work of coaches, players, and management has pushed football to the number one spot in North American sports, but it wasn't always so.

Football has taken 150 years to reach the mass appeal it now enjoys. After several deaths in the early part of the last century, President Theodore Roosevelt threatened to ban football. Cooler heads prevailed, and the sport evolved to become the colossal success it is today. Critics still echo Roosevelt's concerns, but their voices are quickly lost as fans put on their favourite team's jerseys, turn up the volume on their TVs, and analyze the players on their fantasy teams. The game offers some things that humans have always found satisfying. The leadership qualities of great coaches are always a source of interest for fans.

The popularity of football in North America has produced numerous explanations. The game is simple yet complex and intensely physical, yet sound decision-making and finesse often win the day. Team play is crucial as the defence, offence, and special teams operate independently. Defensive, offensive, and special teams create "teams within a team" which can create problems, especially if one unit struggles.

Football teams have relied on numerous slogans and catchphrases to unite their players, such as, "There is no 'I' in team." The Comets, Dinos, Huskies, Eskimos, and Browns faced no such difficulties as they instilled a sense of unity among their players. The coaches and management clearly understood what it takes to create a successful team.

Like all coaches, the exemplary coaches in this book understood that the players needed to buy into a mindset that would make them better tacklers, throwers, blockers, and catchers. But the more important goal for the first families of Alberta football, the Connellans, DeMans, Dudleys, Ivys, and Kadatzes, is that their efforts would benefit their scoreboards and their communities. These programs undoubtedly aimed for championships but did not compromise on values that would produce better citizens.

Whether it be modern-day Alberta, classical Homer's Greece or Shakespeare's England, people have always shared a common goal of improving their communities through stories and activities. Many of these stories are aimed at young people to help produce the kinds of citizens who will be leaders and contributors to the community. People are still mesmerized by the stories of courage and selflessness as the myths lay out what to aim for and what pitfalls to avoid. This book will attempt to do the same through stories highlighting those programs' guiding principles.

The featured teams have provided me with hours of entertainment. With a population of less than 300, Raymond High School holds the most provincial titles and competes against schools approaching ten times their size. Brian Dudley set the table for the Comets' success half a century ago. The Dinos, under Peter Connellan, won four national championships in twelve seasons, and his proteges continue to rack up championships. A young Dennis Kadatz won two consecutive junior football championships in the early 1960s despite being only two years older than some of his Huskies players. The Huskies won a third after Kadatz moved on to the Dinos. Gary DeMan's record as the Browns' coach at St. Francis included fourteen city championships and graduated players who went on to great things with the Dinos and in their communities. During DeMan's run, St. Francis produced seventeen players for the CFL, and fifteen ended up on NCAA rosters. In the 1950s, the Eskimos won three Grey Cups, and some of their players won many more elections in provincial and federal politics. The following pages place these programs on a pedestal they have rightfully earned.

The stories of great teams from Alberta's past and present share five commonalities: a dedication to their communities, tight discipline, a competitive spirit, strong leadership, and embracing diversity when a common goal was agreed upon. Future generations need not look to faraway places for examples of how to bring out the best in people. The motivation and recipe for creating great teams are here in Alberta.

-2-

ACHILLES BLEW IT: DISCIPLINE AND THE SPORTING SPIRIT

On the way back from a victory that propelled the St. Francis Browns into the playoffs, the boys could not wait to start singing their victory song, which they did before they left the parking lot of Shouldice Park. It was 1982, the Browns were 6–0, and their march to a city champion jacket was coming. As the songs progressed into whole-throated, Viking-style chants, the captains introduced minor profanity that is nothing more than what you would hear during an evening of television viewing on the CBC.

The Browns were excited as their hard work and perseverance had paid off as the regular season was over, and now the pursuit of the fabled championship jacket would continue. Coach DeMan quietly asked the driver to pull over several blocks from the stadium and stood to address his team. In the words of Tony Spoletini, it was a moment he wished he could forget as DeMan spoke to the heart of his program and how he had never been so disappointed in a group of young men. Tony recalled his fateful words: "You are undefeated because you are supposed to be undefeated. I am contemplating the forfeiture of our season and not entering the playoffs." DeMan's pronouncement crushed the young men on that bus. Growing up in the communities surrounding St. Francis, all knew the ramifications, including the chance of not wearing the Browns jacket. Only champions were allowed to order football jackets.

Former Brown and now the principal at St. Francis, Luigi Fortini, remembers how Mr. DeMan did not have to raise his voice, but when he had something to say, people listened. Fortini was one of the unfortunate Browns on that bus that day, and it made a lasting impression. DeMan was intimidating, and he was an icon for those young men.

As Spoletini remembered, DeMan got penance as the players arrived at the school and silently moved to the infamous "Hill." The Hill is an incline a few yards south of St. Francis on which generations of Browns have run their conditioning and paid the price for their penalties. Once there, the running began, and it stopped only when the players felt they had atoned for their stupidity.

Coach DeMan recalled how the players used the Hill to remind themselves that some mistakes were inexcusable and that a sacrifice must be made. The Hill was a tradition for rule breakers, and the coaches would watch from their office to see who was redeeming themselves. As Viktor Frankl noted in his book *Man's Search for Meaning*, "In some ways, suffering ceases to be suffering at the moment it finds a meaning, such as the meaning of a sacrifice."

Former Brown, Dino, and CFL running back Chris Lewis recalled the strict protocols after a game: no stopping to chat with parents or girlfriends, one lap around the posts, and no victory celebration until players had left the stadium. This routine was out of respect for the opponents who played courageously in front of their parents and friends. There was no need to humiliate the vanquished further. Compassion for the defeated was essential for DeMan. When the captain started singing too early, a lesson was learned that day.

THE BROWNS' FOUNDING FATHER

Coach DeMan was the only head coach the Browns had ever known. With the formation of the north side school in Calgary, he became the first coach at the school, and he used the opportunity to establish traditions that endured for decades. To this day, if you see someone wearing a Browns jacket, they are a champion. For Coach

DeMan, the jacket symbolizes the sacrifices that champions have to make.

We have much ground to cover before we get to the folly of Achilles, but know that Coach DeMan would have had a lot to say if Achilles were on his team, and if Achilles had listened, that advice might have saved his life. The stakes are high for humans and maybe even higher for those descended from the gods.

Discipline and focus were central to DeMan's process for winning, according to Lewis and Spoletini. Helmets stayed on the whole game. Nobody sat on the bench unless they were talking to a coach. "Discipline, discipline, discipline," Lewis recalled. Spoletini commented that after DeMan left, Joe Stambene, a former player, carried the same traditions forward and had the same success.

St. Francis is a Catholic high school that emphasizes a balanced lifestyle. The foundation of the Catholic Church's love for athletics can be found in the teachings of men like St. Thomas Aquinas (another coach but of a different kind), who felt that games were necessary as there was virtue in moderation. Aquinas felt that working and studying excessively would harm the human spirit. Jesuit teachers quickly incorporated play into the school day. North American Catholic schools excel in many regions, including Alberta. St. Francis and Notre Dame in Calgary, Holy Rosary in Lloydminster, and St. Joseph's in Grand Prairie are perennial contenders for provincial titles.

Good mentorship of young people is the cornerstone of education. Over time, schools have played a significant role in physical, moral, and intellectual development. What used to be shared among churches, schools, and families has increasingly now become the "heavy lifting" of schools alone. Public schools and people like DeMan have taken on a role that society should greatly appreciate.

After observing him coach, Father Whelihan at St. Mary's told Gary his future involved coaching and teaching physical education. This was a total surprise as Gary had a minimal physical education background. Still, the priest valued, like Aquinas, the value of the physical and moral development of young people that DeMan excelled at.

The current St. Francis is quite different from the St. Francis that the Forzanis, Spoletinis, Fortinis, and Geremias attended decades ago. Today's school has several hundred students enrolled as ESL (English as a second language) students. According to Principal Fortini, faith's central role in delivering curriculum and values at the school has never wavered. Bishop McGrattan of Calgary corrected Fortini when he was the Principal at St. Mary two years back when Fortini said that Catholic schools were magical places. McGrattan replied, "It is not magic, Fortini, it is faith!" The Browns still pray before and after games, still run hills, and all students take the mandatory religion classes in grades ten, eleven, and twelve.

Funding pressures make for some hard choices for school boards and principals. The situation at St. Francis is the same, but the emphasis on values and moral education is a ray of light for athletic programming. Fortunately, some decision-makers like Fortini understand and value the role that athletics plays in developing young people.

Let's look back at a bit of history that ties directly to the role of mentorship of young men. A modern-day version of the master-apprentice relationship that dominated Europe during the Middle Ages until the Industrial Revolution of the nineteenth century has yet to appear. In pre-industrial society, young men (usually around age thirteen) were sent to apprentice and live alongside master artisans. There they would learn a trade or a vocation that would eventually lead to a job and provide the basics for a family.

Through his apprenticeship, the young man would learn a career and other valuable life skills. In addition to his craft, the young man may have picked up what it meant to be a husband and father. The apprentice would observe that courage and sensitivity are two characteristics required of husbands and fathers if they, their families, and their communities were to prosper. The courage to learn from mistakes and do the right thing is crucial, as is having the sensitivity to know the feelings of those around you and to act accordingly. Fathers in the Middle Ages were vested in having their sons learn and prosper under another man's guidance to learn these values as eventually they would also be responsible for their parents in their twilight years. The abuse of apprentices was widespread, as it was a much harder world for children in their teens at that period of time. There were few checks on the craftsmen and how they treated those for whom they were responsible.

With the arrival of mass production, the factory replaced the craft industry in Northern Europe. The life lessons learned by the apprentice in the pre-industrial days vanished. The mentorship of young men largely vanished.

Things started to improve for children in Britain when Parliament in Scotland ratified the Education Act of 1633. Close to 200 years before the Industrial Revolution, this revolutionary legislation commanded every parish to establish a public school to increase literacy, which would help facilitate the reading of the Bible. North America and the rest of Britain lagged behind Scotland for nearly two centuries, but in the mid-1800s, public schools became increasingly widespread.

Alongside literacy evolved a high regard for moral education. "Book learning" was one thing, but active learning was also meaningful. Later in the twentieth century, the rise of physical education and interscholastic sports in British public schools (private) became a popular way to realize the teaching of mind, spirit, and body. For a lucky few, the modern equivalent of the apprentice and master re-emerged on the playing field in the relationship between coach and player.

Critics have often questioned the dollars spent on athletics. They point out that budgets are limited and valuable classroom resources are wasted on sports. The ongoing debate over allocating dollars to education can sometimes be decisive in school districts. The impact of positive sports programs is hard to quantify and usually depends on the testimony of educators and students who have experienced the benefits of positive leadership.

Former Victoria High School quarterback Bo Jereniuk remembers former Eskimo Bob Dean's positive influence when Bo was struggling with the demands of university. Bo sought the advice of an academic counsellor who wisely reminded him of Coach Dean's famous three R's—review, repeat, repetition. Those three R's salvaged the former Vic QB's semester and kick-started a career that positively influenced thousands of young men and ladies.

Solutions to community problems often fall into the laps of school boards and their taxpayers. For example, schools have had to assume additional responsibilities in communities where over 50 percent of the families are single-parent households. Many children have lost the benefit of the guidance of two adults in the home.

In communities hit hardest by disruption to the family unit, well-constructed, value-laden athletic programs are greatly beneficial. In inter-school athletics, participants become exposed to the discipline and sacrifice that may or may not be missing in their homes. Practising games teaches the necessity of sacrifice in achieving goals. One school training facility has printed above its doorway: "We Train to Practice, We Practice to Play, We Play to Win!"

The question then becomes, what and where will we impart the messages that young people need to define their roles within their communities and families? Former Brown, Utah State alumni, and Calgary Stampeder Tom Forzani said he had many coaches, but Coach DeMan was most responsible for his success. Many years after having his number retired from the Stampeders, Forzani remarked, "Gary understood adolescents. He knew the buttons to push. He knew the game was to be played competitively and the correct way. Nobody was going to tell me that guy was wrong! Never! He wasn't lucky for thirty years!" Coach DeMan's process was rooted in an intensely competitive atmosphere with strict adherence to his values-laden approach to winning.

The teams highlighted in this book approach mentorship in various ways. As a coach at a post-secondary institution, Peter Connellan applied expectations differently than Coach Bob Dean did at an inner-city school in Edmonton. St. Francis and Raymond had values-laden programs that drew heavily upon their unique communities and circumstances to prepare their players to play and prosper. The Edmonton Huskies of the 1960s were exceptional in the approach taken by their incredibly young staff, and it closely resembled the process Connellan later adopted in Calgary.

COMETS ARE RARE

The Raymond Comets are unique in Alberta athletics. With a school population of fewer than 300 students, it regularly defeats schools several times its size. Most of its students are Latter-Day Saints from more traditional family backgrounds. Single-parent families are a rarity in Raymond, and school discipline problems are few and far between.

As a result, Jim Ralph, a former principal and now school board chairman, described his role much like a Maytag repairman. Jim was referring to the 1980s television marketing strategy by Maytag Appliances, showing a lonely repairman staring at his phone, hoping for service calls.

I am unsure what the international best-selling author Jordan Peterson knows about Raymond football, but he would appreciate their "playbook." Dr. Jordan Peterson says, "Sports are a great analogy for life because life is like a game. Like sports, you are setting forth an aim and arranging your perceptions and actions to pursue that." Peterson, a native of Fairview, Alberta, has sold over seven million books on organizing your life. His *Twelve Rules for Life* has changed hundreds of thousands of lives with his scientific and social insights into personality and communities. Teaching people how to create order out of the chaos of life is Peterson's goal. Coaches aim to do the same with their teams. The Comets and the Browns intentionally use religion as a unifying element that minimizes chaos and distractions.

Raymond has been consistent on how to organize its team to achieve its goals. Coaches Ralph and Dudley did not believe in a long list of rules. At Raymond, players were told, "Our goal is to win provincials, so what do we have to do to get there?" In the program's early years, the players would lay out the rules: "Be good students, no partying, no drinking or drugs." Players wrote out the rules and abided by them. Ralph emphasized that the team is only as strong as the weakest link. "Nobody wants to be that player!"

The Church might as well be the recognized "head coach," as its influence is everywhere in Southern Alberta communities like

Raymond, Magrath, Sterling, and Cardston. The only dry counties in Canada are on seven First Nations reserves and in Raymond. A referendum was held in the spring of 2022 that continued Raymond's practice of prohibiting the sale of alcohol. The "joy" that alcohol brings to many communities is seen by those in Raymond as contributing to the chaos that Peterson describes.

The conservatism of southern Alberta is legendary, and the majority there embraces the "conserve" part of conservatism. It is impossible to separate the success of the Comets from the values that underlie the Church of Jesus Christ of Latter-Day Saints. Discipline plays a vital role in all aspects of church life. Southern Alberta is reluctant to cast aside a way of life that has enabled them to tackle their part of the West.

Brian Dudley of Raymond started the Southern Alberta Football League in 1967. His approach to athletics mirrored the values of the community. As Raymond football's "founding father," he was ultimately responsible for dealing with rule breakers. Dudley's approach was to deal with problems individually and respect the player's dignity. Dudley was not heavy-handed in dealing with the few problems he encountered. He attributed the absence of issues to the positive peer pressure on the team and in the community. "Our religion tells you what is wrong, and if they've done something wrong and you let them know, you know that was usually enough. Discipline is not a big deal in Raymond."

Raymond players never got a break from getting the message. From Monday to Friday, it was football teaching the values, and on Sundays, the Church filled in the blanks. In the mornings, the seminary taught church values before class. The term, "the Program," is sometimes used by church leadership to describe the tenets and discipline required to raise and mentor their youth. Let us take a quick look at the detail that the Church goes into regarding lifestyle and mentoring.

It is difficult to understand Raymond's success without knowing about the teachings of the Latter-Day Saints. I asked many questions about their approach to child raising and received direct answers with few surprises. To shed some light on the Church and its role in its members' lives, we will draw on Blair Bennett, an LDS leader who achieved the rank of seventy in the Church hierarchy. Blair was responsible for 125 stakes of 8–15 wards, each with 350–400 members. Blair is an avid sportsman and expert on how to raise youth through athletics and the Program. For young people, the Church is clear on priorities. Church leaders view athletics as an excellent way to keep young people's focus on positive habits and avoid the problems of having idle hands and little direction.

The extent to which LDS youth will accept direction from the church hierarchy is seen in the Program regarding finding a life partner. First, you date, then you court, and if that goes well, you get engaged, then you get married, and only *then* do you have intimate relations. Ultimately, having a family is the goal of married couples. For Latter-Day Saints, the Program is communicated honestly to young people who appreciate straight talk. Self-discipline is key in most aspects of church doctrine, and it is no different in sports.

CHURCH AND ATHLETICS

Athletics is important, as church doctrine believes the spirit and the body unite to create the soul. Most people are familiar with the church doctrine that discourages caffeine use. Still, the Church endorses many other dietary habits, such as eating whole grains, vegetables, and fruit. Proper rest and exercise are also encouraged, as the body is fundamental in nurturing the soul. Sports, dance, and the Program all fit the bigger picture of a good life and a better after-life. As Bennett believes, "Stand for something. Teach the Program."

Active teens, the Church believes, have less time to find themselves in compromising situations that could detract from a healthy lifestyle. There is a saying the Church uses that resonates with young people: "Dark, tired, late, and alone." For Bennett, this is a recipe for problems, and young people must control at least three of the four ingredients in that recipe to avoid trouble. The clarity that church doctrine provides leaves little room for interpretation or experimentation.

The Church's Saturday night dances are organized and have a specific purpose within the Program. For most teenage boys, asking a young lady to dance is no easy feat. Resiliency is a quality that the Church nourishes in its young men and women. Young men are taught courage and the ability to recover after setbacks. Girls at around age sixteen are educated as to the vulnerability of boys. They are taught to empathize with boys when they approach them to dance. The point is to teach compassion on the part of the girls and how the answer, "Yes, I'd love to," helps build the confidence of young men to take risks. The Church's thinking is that young men who are willing to take a chance when failure is possible make better teammates and community members.

Socrates's famous "Know thyself" calls people to know where they fit in society. Church elders inform their boys that girls who may or may not be interested will accept an invitation to dance, but on the second or third request, she has the right to decline. If she accepts on the third request, she may be interested in the young man. Another way that girls control the situation is by using their left hand to control the distance between them and their partners. If they relax their hand, it sends a message to the boy that they are interested. As teenagers, this communicates respect, which should transfer to other situations in their lives.

LDS churches are community gathering places and almost always have a gym. Year-round sports have been encouraged in the last couple of decades in Raymond where football and baseball have gained on the status of basketball. It is no coincidence that the basketball court on Saturday becomes the dance floor in the evening. The Program is relentless, and when the rich tradition of winning is added, the recipe for championships is complete.

Coaches from towns in southern Alberta have a smaller base from which to draw athletes, but their talent pool is focused. In the larger urban centres of Alberta, the number of athletes is proportionately larger but not necessarily as focused. The distractions and alternative activities in cities are obvious, as are the conflicting views on how much guidance children need.

DISCIPLINE, DISCIPLINE, DISCIPLINE . . .

As mentioned earlier, discipline issues were rarely a problem with the Comets. Lack of commitment, work pressure, demands from other sports, lack of discipline, putting "me" before "we," attendance concerns, and a lack of parental support are the reality for most coaches, but not in Raymond.

Raymond's Jim Ralph's voice cracked as he commented on how fortunate his community is: "We are so naïve as to how the rest of the world operates. We can hardly understand how some kids come with so much baggage and little support." As Ralph learned that one inner-city football program in Edmonton had twenty-seven of thirty boys living in homes without fathers, he sadly shook his head. Student teachers in Raymond were warned early by administrators that their experience probably would not be the reality for the rest of their careers.

How coaches in other centres deal with these issues is an exciting study of the necessity of coaches being true to themselves and their values. What worked for former Edmonton Eskimo, Rollie Miles, at St. Joseph's in Edmonton in the 1960s and 1970s may differ from the approach of Gary DeMan in Calgary or Bob Dean in Edmonton's inner city. Still, all three were successful. Good coaches find a way, and it is *their way*, whatever the obstacles or challenges.

Victoria Composite High School in the 1960s had a population larger than the town of Raymond. The athletes available at a large school are usually proportional to their large population. But Raymond had young men who dreamed of being Comets as young boys and were supported by the community in that respect. Coach Dean had a much different task: building mindsets and athletes with little support and background in sports.

Coach Dean had many experiences and mentors that influenced his coaching. In the 1950s, Canadian professional football was almost on economic par with the NFL. The CFL could attract athletes like Jackie Parker, Rollie Miles, Art Walker, and John Bright, and coaches from premier college programs. Men like Darrell Royal and Pop Ivy with ties to the University of Oklahoma were happy to come to Alberta and coach the Eskimos.

One can only speculate on Coaches Darrell Royal and Pop Ivy's (Eskimos coaches from the 1950s) effect on Bob Dean and his teammates. Many Eskimos later ventured into coaching, and the success they enjoyed as players continued as mentors. Great teams focus on fundamentals, have superior athletes, and have a thorough playbook understanding. Former Eskimos experienced that while playing under Ivy and Royal.

Many of the 1950s Eskimos, notably Bob Dean, Rollie Miles, and Johnny Bright, were successful coaches. Other Eskimos did it in the workplace or business. They all seemed to bring out the best in people. The "soft skills" of building relationships are challenging to explain, but the 1950s Eskimos seemed to understand team building. The Eskimos' positive effect on the community left a larger legacy than their three consecutive Grey Cup victories.

Coach Dean would have also used lessons from his youth. Born and raised in Steeltown, his later experiences in the Korean War must have significantly impacted his character development. His subsequent experiences on highly successful football teams at the University of Maryland and at the pro level would have served to apply earlier experiences to the game of football.

Blue-collar towns with large immigrant workforces bring young people together from diverse backgrounds. Players from different cultures and who spoke other languages needed the common language of discipline to succeed. In many ways, Victoria Composite High School resembled Pittsburgh's diverse population. In describing Dean's approach to discipline, I was struck by how different it was from the process used by the Dinos, Comets, and Browns. Different situations demand unique approaches, and Victoria Composite was one of those places.

Bohdan Jereniuk, a player at Victoria in the 1960s, defined Dean's approach to discipline as "F and I": fear and intimidation. Victoria Composite's inner-city cast of vocational and first-generation Canadian students did not have a common faith or values governing their lives. They did not have a common first language, as many were first- or second-generation Canadians from postwar Europe. Dean must have felt a sense of urgency in bringing order to his young students' lives.

Vic players had parents who often worked two or three jobs to make ends meet and who had little time to monitor their boys' co-curricular activities. Dean understood that he would often have to be the de facto father figure in his players' lives and that football would be the way to channel the boys' energy in a positive manner. Bo recalled his father telling Coach Dean that because he spent more time with Bo, he could discipline him however he saw fit.

Jereniuk remarked that when Dean became principal, he always had the last word on discipline. Principal Dean always accompanied the teams on their trips to the US. On one trip, one player was caught intoxicated after curfew. The rules were obvious, but Bob said, "We will suspend him when we return." Bo reminded Bob that the first game back was challenging, so Bob said, "Okay, the second game, we will teach him a lesson!" The boy appreciated the chance to play, and many years later he became a great community member and neighbour of the Jereniuks.

When he was a coach at Victoria Composite, Dean was aware of the players' varied backgrounds. Edmonton's Boyle Street area produced many Vic players with stories that reflect the rough and tumble community. One player was forced to work to help his single mother provide for his family's necessities. As a result, the young man's attendance suffered. Coach Dean refused to succumb to teacher pressure to bench the boy, and as George Paleniuk recalls, the team knew that Dean was correct and respected him for his decision.

Dean's uncompromising approach to discipline did not stop him from acting according to the situation and doing what was right. Pop Ivy, his Eskimos coach, had similar flexibility in dealing with the mischievous characters on his teams. If, as Shakespeare thought, the measure of a man is his capacity for courage and sensitivity, then Dean modelled that definition in how he took the time to understand his players.

Bob Dean, like many coaches, had little time for players thinking that their teams were true democracies where they had a voice. The players chose to join the team and had to abide by the rules. Bullies on his teams soon learned that Dean had no problem using his reputation and size to intimidate them.

Bo Jereniuk remembers how Dean would walk straight toward bullies in his hallways and physically ram them if they refused to yield to him. Jereniuk recalled that Dean always made it look like an accident, but the message was clear: "These hallways and this team answers to me." Dean's reputation in turning around schools that needed it was legendary in the Edmonton public school system.

George Paleniuk remembered a disgruntled veteran in Vic bullying younger players because Coach Dean wasn't letting him play the position he wanted. In one practice, the veteran was incredibly abusive toward a young player and warranted Dean's warning: "If you do that again, you will get my foot up your ass." Unfortunately, the player continued with his stupidity, and the coach's response was what the coach described. The offending player quickly got over his problem with the new position he was assigned and became much more manageable. Men who have experienced combat understand human nature in a way that the authors of textbooks do not.

CHANNELLING AGGRESSION

Rough play provides healthy outlets for youngsters. Games have a huge purpose in our socialization. Several decades ago, a blunder occurred in Quebec when authorities did not tolerate rough play in daycares. The goal was to create kinder, gentler children who would grow into adulthood with less disagreeable characteristics. Several years later, they reversed this policy as the boys became unmanageable. Without an outlet for their need for rough play, there were negative changes in the personalities of these children.

Controlled aggression in contact sports is often criticized but may be infinitely safer than the alternatives adolescents might seek whenever and wherever they can find them. The consequences of driving fast, getting into fights, petty and not-so-petty thefts, vandalism, and drug use can be life-altering for young people.

Some critics maintain that the injuries suffered in contact sports justify cancelling those activities. Others say sports like football encourage aggression and competitiveness, leading to violent crime, conflict, and even war. Luckily, there is no shortage of psychologists and lay people with a clearer understanding of human nature who understand the need for humans to find a physical means as an outlet for aggressive impulses. Football's response to the criticisms is to keep evolving the rules to enhance player safety while maintaining the game's competitiveness and aggressive nature.

Injuries will occur regardless of the gains made in rule changes to facilitate player safety. Blocking below the waist, targeting the head, and hitting the QB below the waist have all been rule infractions. In their drive to quell the rising tide of permanent head injuries, concussion research led by the NFL has paved the way for better teaching practices and rule changes in all sports where head injuries occur.

Teachers and coaches know that boys and girls are similar regarding aggression in many ways but different in others. Channelling aggression in young people has challenged parents and communities since the beginning. Elder wisdom in channelling aggression is even more critical today as the stakes appear higher.

CONNELLAN'S GENIUS

Peter Connellan's insight and respect for human dignity and the role that sacrifice and discipline play in evolving that value through sport is an exciting study. His record and the number of championships he won speak loudly to his winning formula. If he were an American coach with his record, his likeness would be gracing a statue outside McMahon Stadium today. The on- and off-field excellence that the Dinos reached under Connellan is seldom seen in sports.

Coach Connellan started coaching at Old Scona in Edmonton while attending the University of Alberta. He was fortunate to have played hockey under the legendary Clare Drake and to have experienced the mentorship of men like Murray Smith and Maury Van Vliet. The University of Alberta in the 1950s had an enormous impact on athletics across Canada.

Connellan started a program at Innisfail High School upon graduation before moving to the Calgary Public School Board. Eventually, he joined the University of Calgary in 1983. In his first year, he won a Vanier Cup. The standards set by Connellan and his assistants were well known in Calgary football circles.

The Dinos' head coach's magic in asserting himself while building attachments or relationships with his players employed the same logic the Chinese general, Sun Tzu, used 2,500 years ago. "If soldiers are punished before they have grown attached to you, they will not prove submissive, and, unless submissive, then they will be practically useless." As an educator, Connellan knew that relationship building was the cornerstone of his program. Legendary Chinese generals and Alberta's football coaches have many things in common.

Connellan may never have needed to read Sun Tzu, but three-time Super Bowl Champion and Hall of Fame coach Bill Walsh of the San Francisco 49ers did. Walsh referred to Sun Tzu's *The Art of War* as a source for strategic and motivational purposes. Walsh's admission moved *The Art of War* onto the *New York Times* Best Seller list. Human nature, geography, and tactics have not changed much in the 3,000 years since *The Art of War* was written.

Connellan included a healthy dose of humour, which lightened the mood when things became difficult. A former Dino fondly described the Dinos' coaching staff as "failed comedians." After a loss in Saskatchewan, Tony Spoletini, star fullback, remembers the bus stopping in Kindersley, SK. Tony used the opportunity to pick up a few treats to ease the pain of losing to the Huskies of Saskatoon. Spoletini returned carrying a bag loaded with high-fat, sugar-filled treats that required the support of both hands. As Tony passed by Coach Connellan's seat at the front of the bus, Connellan's voice stopped him in his tracks. "Tony, how much do you weigh?"

"I'm, uh, two-twenty, Coach."

"No, more like two-forty, Tony. Let me see what's in the bag."

As Connellan rummaged through the bag doing an inventory, he grew increasingly agitated with Tony's disregard for dietary discipline. Much to Tony's dismay, the contents were dispersed to his teammates. Coach Connellan added insult to injury with the remark that Tony looked a step slower in Saskatoon and that there would be a weigh-in on Monday.

The trip home from Saskatoon was a constant barrage by Tony's teammates taking advantage of his misfortune as he pressed his face to the window and watched the prairies roll by. The ribbing was relentless as they let him know how slow he looked. Maybe he had lost a step, and perhaps it was good that his treat bag had been confiscated.

At the Monday weigh-in, Tony was 220, not 240, but no apology was forthcoming. All players, stars or backups, were expected to be accountable and dedicated to excellence. Nobody escaped the scrutiny, wit, or wrath of the former principal and now head coach.

Connellan left nothing to chance, and he communicated his expectations to players and coaches. In Connellan's words, he "flooded the players" with the same messages on paper every year. Connellan told players they controlled the locker room. Coaches came under the same scrutiny. "I don't want to see you talking to the kids in practice," he'd say. "I want to see them running drills!" Connellan forewarned his coaches, telling them, "If I stepped into a drill to correct, I didn't want a discussion with players or the unit coach about why they were doing it a certain way. It was to be done the agreed-upon way!" There was a time for discussions, but the field was not that place.

Molson sponsored the Dinos football team and provided refreshments for the road trips home. At the infamous Kindersley stop, halfway between Calgary and Saskatoon, Lewis and a friend ran to the local hotel to get a couple more cases as they had run out of beer on the bus. "Coach Connellan said nothing as we walked by him on the bus, but the next day he called us in and said, 'At no time did I permit you to buy extra beers.' He sat us down for the first quarter of the next game. We were expected to learn from our mistakes. Good coaches give you a chance to do that."

ACCOUNTABILITY KEY FOR DINOS

The TEAM (together everybody achieves more) philosophy and influence extended to everyone involved in the program. Players, coaches, and support staff all had mutually agreed upon roles. All were accountable, but when Connellan's rules were broken, the intent was to change the behaviour, not punish the person. Sports Information Hall of Fame member (and the only Canadian ever inducted) Jack Neumann recalled the time he made the mistake of picking the Dinos nominee for university player of the week without consulting the head coach. As he passed the office on that unfortunate day, Peter asked Jack to join him and to "shut the door behind you."

Jack knew Pete well enough that "shut the door behind you" was not promising. Connellan told Jack that his choice for player of the week cost the Dinos an interception, as he ran an incorrect route, and a QB sack, as he didn't recognize the coverage, and that he was not a good choice or even his "damn choice." At that point, he grabbed the submission form and advised Jack that he (Connellan), not Jack, would be making these decisions, then ripped the nomination into three pieces, which ended up in the trash. Neumann ended the story with, "The tremendous success of the Dinos in the eighties owed *everything* to Connellan's leadership abilities."

Chris Lewis, a former Dino and CFL running back, recalled a film session when he was a rookie and had made a mistake. "He got his highlighter and said, 'Lewis, you are supposed to be here! Don't you know where you are supposed to be?'" Rather than be accountable, Lewis said yes, that he was sorry, but that it was his first year. "I don't give a damn if it's your first year," Connellan said. "If you're on the field, you're expected to perform!" Lewis added, "Peter would never have allowed a player to dictate anything to him!"

Spoletini talked about the intensity of two-a-days in the fall camp, where by day four, "You could hardly feel your body." Coach Connellan would hit in the morning and afternoon practices and keep the intensity at a fever pitch for several days. As the going got tough, more players would escape to the trainer's room or the sidelines. Player leaders Wade Buteau and John Harvey would preach that it was time to "man up" as they were hurt, not injured. Connellan, like the Huskies and the Comets, leaned heavily on his leaders.

Keith Holliday, Dinos linebacker in 1983, said that on the road, "We never had to worry about missed curfews or drinking the night before a game. The guys were committed to getting the win. Coaches were never cruising hotel hallways or doing bed checks. We were treated like men, but it was a different story after the game."

Holliday added, "The root of Connellan's thing was not so much to manage you but get you to get your act together. 'Do you want to do this? This is how we will do this; now it is up to you.'" Testing on the first day would identify who was ready to win a championship. Connellan and his staff insisted on accountability and self-discipline.

Dino Coaching Legends (L-R) Tony Fasano, Dennis Kadatz,
Wayne Harris Jr, Mike Lashuk and Peter Connellan

ARE YOU HURT OR INJURED?

The structure and discipline of exemplary programs provide youth with a blueprint for future success. Ultimately, these programs, through their steps to promote player leadership, produce citizens who, upon entering their communities as adults, will have had experience building teams and finding solutions.

Dallas Cowboy and NFL Hall of Famer Roger Staubach said this about resiliency: "All of us get knocked down. But it's resiliency that matters. All of us do well when things are going well, but what distinguishes athletes is the ability to do well in times of great stress, urgency, and pressure."

Parents, like coaches, have to decide very early in their children's lives how to protect their children. In doing so, they may get hurt physically and/or fathom the grim reality that, in their present state, they may not be the next Albert Einstein, Tom Brady, or Steve Jobs. Today, we use terms like "helicopter parents" or "bulldozer parents" negatively because our psyche knows those types do their children few favours. The children of a society that values coddling may be safer but not stronger.

Young coaches often need more life experience to understand that the primary lesson that can be learned from sports is accountability. The standard for personal accountability on championship teams is almost beyond reach. Protecting athletes from taking ownership of their mistakes takes many forms. Blaming referees, weather conditions, or lousy luck may make players feel better, but they are being done a disservice.

A NOT-SO-BIG CITY BECKONED

When future CFL Hall of Famer Norm Kimball left the Edmonton Huskies in 1964 to work with the Edmonton Eskimos, the Huskies board of directors handed over the coaching reins to a twenty-two-year-old graduate of the program named Dennis Kadatz. Kadatz was raised on a farm a few miles south of Edmonton. During his high school years, his parents purchased a home near Mill Creek Ravine where he and his sister Marlene lived while they attended Strathcona High School. A stand-out player in high school, Dennis graduated from the Huskies, where he, like Connellan, benefitted from the teaching of Murray Smith. Smith later became an essential part of Dennis's post-secondary education as a professor of sports psychology in the Faculty of Physical Education at the University of Alberta.

Kadatz's record with the Edmonton Huskies etched him forever in Edmonton's sports history, with national championships in 1962 and 1963 before leaving for the University of Alberta in Calgary as the coach of their fledgling program. In 1964, the team won a third championship with one of Kadatz's assistants, Joe Hutton, leading the team to victory over the Montreal Maple Leafs at McMahon Stadium. According to the *Edmonton Journal* (Nov. 10, 1964), the eastern champions outweighed the Huskies by twenty-five pounds per man.

At age twenty-two and recently married to his young wife Denise, Kadatz found himself a local hero as a national champion coach while working on his master's degree in physical education. Denise and Dennis made a formidable team, as both were graduates of the University of Alberta and had football backgrounds. Denise grew up on the south side of Edmonton, and her family included her brother and Huskies star Rod Esper.

Denise Kadatz was integral in the accomplishments of her life partner. Whether it be as a sounding board for important decisions, raising a family, entertaining International Olympic Committee dignitaries, renovating properties, or being a partner to her husband's vision, Denise was up to the task. Her memories of the Huskies championships and the Calgary Olympics are full of gratitude for the time she had with Dennis and their many accomplishments.

The early 1960s was a very different time for young married women. Denise, a University of Alberta Faculty of Education graduate, laughingly recalled how pregnant women who began to "show" were discreetly removed from the classroom. Who knows how that tradition of keeping children safe from the knowledge of the "birds and bees" helped the Kadatz partnership rise to such lofty heights?

Liverpool had their Fab Four in 1962, but Edmonton had Kadatz's national champion Huskies. The *Edmonton Journal*'s account of the reception the Huskies received after winning their first Dominion title sounded much like what The Beatles received on their first tour of America. Huskies mania swept Edmonton on Nov. 27, 1962 after Trans-Canada Air Lines safely delivered the Huskies home.

The Huskies were whisked from the airport, where hundreds of fans met them at Jubilee Auditorium. "With close to a thousand fans jamming the lower rotunda of the auditorium, the Huskies were met by the rousing strains of 'You Gotta Be a Football Hero' by the Tailgate Jazz Band and received congratulations from a battery of speakers. Heading the list was J. Percy Page, the lieutenant governor." So said the Nov. 27, 1962 issue of the *Edmonton Journal*.

The road to the Jubilee Auditorium was long. It started several years before with the hiring of Murray Smith and the club's transition from the Southside Oilers to the Edmonton Huskies. The lofty expectations set by Murray Smith inspired his proteges to carry on the tradition of excellence he set. The Huskies' youthful coaching staff continued to set high standards on and off the field. The itinerary set for the Western final in 1962 outlined this example. The last sentence is like lightning: "Behave like the men we know you are and don't forget what we came for." They aimed to win and they did.

There is No Substitution for Preparation.

Pack in duffle bag—hip pads, shoulder pads, thigh pads, knee pads, helmet and chin strap, game pants and game socks, game sweater, towel, and belt.

Pack in a carry bag—shoes, socks, sweat pants, jock, sweatshirt, and towel.

Team Regulations

1. Always be on Time—Don't hold the rest of the team up.
2. A shirt, tie, and jacket are to be worn at all times in public.
3. Anyone consuming alcohol or anyone late for curfew will not dress on Sunday.
4. Remember who you are and who you are representing. Behave like the men we know you are, and don't forget what we came here for.

Due partly to the slight age difference between Kadatz and his players, they remained a tight group that enjoyed yearly reunions in Kelowna where stories were told and small wagers were made. Many stories' inspiration came from the remarkable leadership of the Huskies' coaches, players, and administrators. One of the most inspirational players in Huskies history was Bob Bateman from the southside.

Later, Kadatz called Bateman the most outstanding leader he had ever seen on and off the field, but it didn't stop Kadatz from doing the unthinkable and sending his leader off the field. George Spanach, a player and future CFLer, on the three-peat team, remarked, "Coach had us in the palm of his hand." He described one practice when they ran a pulling guard drill involving several players in a high-collision situation. Spanach recalled Kadatz voicing his frustration that the drill wasn't being run with the necessary intensity and told Bateman "to take his gear and get off the field." Bateman quietly left without protest, and a silence fell over the practice field.

For casual observers, Coach Kadatz's actions may seem extreme. His genius was his willingness to tell everyone that no one was above the team's standards. Everyone was accountable. Coaches often give the best athletes a free pass for not reaching their potential. When such standards are compromised, mediocrity wins and excellence suffers.

Kadatz had given the boot to Bobby Bateman, the heart and soul of the Edmonton Huskies. The stillness of the North Saskatchewan River valley was soon broken by the Huskies resuming the drill with a sense of purpose. Another Huskie, Marv Roberts, recalled that the sound of helmets and shoulder pads colliding was tenfold as Bateman left the field. It seemed the only way they could protest his loss was to show Kadatz their respect for him and any decision he had to make. Another aspect of the players' reaction may have been their desperation to please their coach so they could regain their captain.

Why Bateman was punished was unclear, but Coach Kadatz was resolute. Maybe he was telling his veterans they were responsible for the intensity of practice. Bateman returned the next day with the expectation raised for his leadership. If he could not recognize poor effort and then correct it, he was accountable. So was Kadatz, who was ultimately responsible for the team's success. If he refused to act, he was not taking responsibility as the coach.

Sixty years after meeting Bateman for the first time, many of his teammates' voices soften and sometimes waver as they recall their friend's impact on their lives. For many of them, he was their best friend. An undersized lineman, Bateman possessed great technique. He also personified two essential components of leadership: compassion and hard work. Great teams have great leaders, and Bateman was one of those. In fact, many called him the best they had ever seen. For Kadatz to send Bateman into that locker room was a message that was not soon forgotten, and it stayed with those who witnessed it for sixty years.

When the Browns celebrated in front of a vanquished foe in the early 1980s, Coach DeMan's message was similar to the one Kadatz sent by throwing Bateman off the practice field. Men like Kadatz and DeMan embodied long-held beliefs surrounding character. A team's ruin could stem from unsportsmanlike behaviour. Celebrations we see today after touchdowns are scored, passes are intercepted or even when tackles are made are me-centred, ego-driven mistakes.

The best teammates acknowledge the person who assisted on their goal, basket, or touchdown. Some point to the heavens as if divine intervention made the block to get them to the endzone, not the bloodied and battered lineman. Others pound their chest as if they were solely responsible for the play.

HOMER WARNED US

Three thousand years ago, the Greek poet Homer had lots to say about the mistakes humans should try to avoid. His epics, *The Iliad* and *The Odyssey*, tell of a Greek campaign against the city of Troy in what is now Turkey. Homer's influence on western civilization can still be seen today as many of our ideas around what constitutes a good life trace their roots to the blind Greek poet.

If the leader of the Greek invasion force that invaded Troy, Agamemnon, had been able to rein in his famous hero, Achilles might have survived that epic battle. Agamemnon's failure to change his mindset was tragic for Achilles.

When Homer wrote *The Iliad* and *The Odyssey*, he had a lot to say about men's defects and noble qualities. Achilles's many emotional tirades came close to unnecessarily tipping the balance in favour of the Trojans. After the death of his distant cousin Patroclus, Achilles defies his immortal mother, Thetis, who warns him that if he takes revenge on Hector, he will be killed. With the battle for Troy in the balance, Achilles elevates his guilt for not protecting Patroclus above the effort to take Troy. Achilles was famous for his pouty behaviour when things did not go his way. He posed a dilemma for the Greek commanders as his fighting abilities were legendary, but he was unpredictable and lacked sensitivity toward his allies. Battle allowed men like Achilles to gain accolades and immortality through their deeds. Homer's characterization of Achilles is a story that resonates throughout the ages, but as entertaining as it is, it is also a warning.

Homer offered up Odysseus as a better example of the kind of male Greeks should aspire to become. Odysseus's goal was a victory for his army so he could return to a peaceful life at home with his loved ones. For Odysseus, war was an obligation and a service to his community that had to be fulfilled. Personal accolades mattered little to the Greek hero.

With the Greeks running out of supplies and patience in their siege of Troy, a council was called, including the leaders who approved of Odysseus's plan to fake a retreat back to Greece and leave a gift of a large wooden horse filled with warriors. Odysseus hoped the Trojans would take the gift behind the city walls, and when their victory party ended, the Greeks would sneak out of the horse and open the gates for the Greeks who had secretly stayed behind. The plan worked and in the ensuing battle, the Greeks seized Troy.

Homer recognized and immortalized Odysseus's brilliance, ingenuity, and inspirational leadership. Thanks to Homer, countless generations have admired this sensitive and courageous hero. When Odysseus returned from Troy, the god Poseidon presented him with many challenges for blinding his son Polyphemus. The trip back to his home island of Ithaca required all of the traits that Homer admired in men: bravery, sensitivity, and intellect. Homer set a standard for future generations of men and women.

Homer recognized the bravery of Hector. When he took the field against the Greek champion Achilles, Homer detailed how Hector was sure he would not live to see his wife and child again. For Hector, it was about honour and the need to protect his brother from annihilation at the hands of Achilles. Achilles was a fearless, savage warrior who had little time for the gods or religious conventions. The Greek hero's brashness was beyond even the control of the Greek leader Agamemnon, and when Achilles challenged Hector to come out and fight for the honour of Troy, there was little anyone could do to stop him.

Achilles prevailed in a well-fought battle with the Trojan hero but did himself no favours with how he acted in victory. Achilles killed Hector as his family watched, which added to the tragedy. Hector's heroic death immortalized his actions and showed a side of Achilles that was less than heroic. Homer had little sympathy for Achilles's actions and let it be known. Homer also noted the cowardice of Hector's brother, Paris, as not only did he steal Helen away from her rightful husband, but he also did not take his place on the battlefield against the Greek champion. Paris was no match for Achilles, and Hector's death resulted from his brother's moral and physical cowardice.

Achilles's mistake was what happened when Hector's spirit left his body. While Hector lay dead, Achilles pierced the area between the tendon and the heel with a spear and ran a rope through it, which he tied to his chariot. Then he dragged the dead Trojan hero around the walled city several times as the inhabitants watched and grieved. Among the spectators were Hector's parents, Paris, and

Hector's grieving widow. To add further insult, Achilles refused to leave Hector's body for a proper burial. Hector's father was forced to secretly enter the Greek encampment and beg Achilles for his son's body.

Achilles's days were numbered after the defilement of Hector's body as his actions angered the god Apollo, who vowed revenge. Actions of humans, then and now, can carry grave consequences, and Achilles paid the ultimate price when Paris shot him in the heel with an arrow. Homer insinuated that Apollo guided the arrow that killed Achilles. Some claim that Achilles's lack of humility and disregard for the gods made Paris's aim more concentrated and accurate. The ancient lessons in Homer's epics speak to truths that continue to serve individuals and communities well.

The eternal truths that coaches in this book taught and still teach swirl around the values of community, discipline, sacrifice, team, leadership, diversity, and competition. What better way for young people to learn these essential values than through a game that simultaneously offers competitors companionship and fun?

Discipline remains central to a team's success. Alberta's good teams had an unusually high standard of excellence that stressed personal and group discipline. As St. Thomas Aquinas believed, the justification for play is not only for lessons learned but also to have fun. In our next section, you will see that Alberta's best teams were imbued with hard-working characters who uplifted their teammates' spirits by being humourous and eternally optimistic. The great teams, although disciplined, had lots of fun that fired their spirits long after they took off their jerseys.

-3-

LAUGHING TOGETHER, SUCCEEDING TOGETHER

Before the October 20, 1951, game between the Drake Bulldogs and Oklahoma A&M, the A&M college paper, the *Daily O'Collegian*, predicted that Drake's running back, Johnny Bright, would not finish the game. The newspaper's sources were A&M players and staff. Bright had had an exceptional season and was a favourite to win the Heisman Trophy, an award given to the USA's top college player. It was not only Bright's offensive brilliance that earned the attention of A&M players. It was the running back's skin colour.

Bright was knocked unconscious three times by A&M defensive tackle Wilbanks Smith. The game was barely seven minutes old when Smith's elbow broke Bright's jaw. Still, he completed a sixty-one-yard pass to Jim Pilkington several plays later. Smith's cheap shots were punctuated by racial slurs from his teammates and coaches.

Bright left soon afterward and Drake went down in defeat, 27–14. With A&M coaches, fans, and players still yelling racial slurs, Bright and the Bulldogs left the field in disgust. Bright remembers his teammates being discouraged by the fanaticism of A&M in stopping him from finishing the game. The Bulldogs could do little, as the rules meant nothing to the A&M players.

The Johnny Bright incident became famous. A sequence of photos published in *Life* magazine depicting Smith's first hit on the Drake player grabbed the attention of North America. The overt racism in the images and storyline was startling. Many believed *Life*'s decision to run the photos played a part in swaying public opinion toward supporting the civil rights movement in the USA.

The two photographers—John Robinson and Don Ultang—set up a camera before the game to focus on Bright, as they had heard rumours surrounding him not finishing the game. When Bright left the game injured, Ultang got the film to Des Moines and had it developed. Later, they said they were lucky the incident happened so early, as they only planned to stay until halftime. The incident, which captured the attention of America, may have also helped Bright's decision to snub the Philadelphia Eagles, who picked him in the first round, and sign with the Stampeders in Calgary.

The seven photos won the two photographers a Pulitzer Prize. Smith and Bright were front and centre as race relations gripped America. The drama and the historical setting of this drama in Stillwater is forgotten today, but one wonders about the attention it would have received if Bright had stayed in the USA to play professional football.

No disciplinary action was brought against Oklahoma A&M, and Drake University pulled out of the Missouri Conference. Later, Bradley University joined Drake and quit the conference too. It wasn't until 2003, twenty years after Bright's death, that Oklahoma State President David J. Schmidly wrote a letter to Drake's president, David Maxwell, officially apologizing for Smith's racially motivated attack.

Oklahoma A&M is now Oklahoma State and recently featured two Albertan athletes named Chuba Hubbard from Sherwood Park and Amen Ogbongbemiga from Notre Dame in Calgary. As of 2023, both are playing in the NFL following their careers as Cowboys at Oklahoma State. The irony of two young black men from Bright's hometown playing for Oklahoma State is striking.

UNSTOPPABLE BRIGHT

The Stillwater experience did not stop Bright from having a great career and being voted into the Canadian Football Hall of Fame. Bright's sense of humour and optimism served him well as a teacher and administrator with the Edmonton public school system. The Wilbanks Smiths of the world had little impact on Bright's quest to improve his community.

Team cohesiveness has a therapeutic effect on its members. The unity of purpose and friendship that those 1950s Eskimos experienced transcended race. Everyone benefited from the interactions between teammates from different backgrounds. Edmonton was far from the diverse community it is today, and those players set the stage for the future.

Bright's personality was hardly that of a victim and brought to mind the reflections of Holocaust survivor Viktor Frankl: "To suffer unnecessarily is masochistic rather than heroic." Bright was heroic. A former player on Bright's Bonnie Doon Lancers, Blair Bennett remembers the zest for life that surrounded Bright as he walked the halls of Bonnie Doon. Bright was forever in the gym, yelling at some guy about to take a shot and betting him a milkshake he would miss. Former students and players lovingly remembered Bright for never paying off or receiving payment for the bets he won. Dr. Gary Smith of the U of A played Bright regularly. "I was the leading scorer on the Bonnie Doon team and used to play him for a quarter and sometimes beat him, but he'd never pay!"

Bennett recalled that Bright had a remarkable memory and was a great kidder. Several years later while playing ball, he noticed Bright watching the game from his car. At the end of the game, Bennett approached the car, and before he could introduce himself, Bright raised his hand and stopped him. "*Binniit*—I haven't kicked your butt in years!"

"He made us all feel like we were buddies, and we loved him," Bennett remarked.

Bob Dean was unaware of any team that got along on and off the field as well as the 1950s Green and Gold. Vince Lombardi would have readily identified with the feeling in the Eskimos' locker room, as the Packers players were renowned for their commitment to each other. After one of the Packers' Super Bowl victories, a reporter asked Lombardi his secret. The reporters covering the press conference were probably expecting a trick play or some other form of magic. Instead, Lombardi replied, "They did it because they loved one another."

HUSKIES COACH AND LORD STANLEY

Organizations understand the value of relationships, yet the formula for making relationships happen is complex and hard to achieve. The Edmonton Oilers of the 1980s are one of the greatest teams in sports history, but their path to greatness took time as they suffered many setbacks. With so many stars and led by two of the greatest players in NHL history, the fanbase and the players were desperate for a Stanley Cup, but GM/Coach Glen Sather knew they needed to approach the game as a team.

Sather brought in Dr. Murray Smith from the University of Alberta to identify the issues limiting the Oilers' obvious potential. Smith was a first-rate junior football coach with the Edmonton Huskies and Alberta Golden Bears, but this was the NHL and the stakes were much higher. Sather was desperate and took a chance on the professor.

Dr. Smith's recipe for building a Hall of Fame NHL team was simple. It wasn't any different from the formula he laid out for the Edmonton Huskies and his captain Dennis Kadatz in the late 1950s. Smith's plan for the Oilers had worked for years with Bears coach Clare Drake, a future Canadian Hockey Hall of Famer. The University of Alberta's famed athletic program served as a laboratory for sound practices and impacted the Oilers to a great extent.

Dr. Murray Smith had an illustrious career as a professor and sports psychologist. According to Mark Messier and Wayne Gretzky, Smith was essential in melding the Oilers into a team. They recalled meeting Smith for the first time and wondering aloud what he could offer a professional hockey team. The Oilers stars soon changed their minds, however, as Smith worked through his message of "team first." On many occasions, former Oilers spoke of the mantra that Smith, Drake, and Kadatz preached: "That it was remarkable what could be achieved when nobody cared who got the credit." The young Oilers needed help, and they found it in Dr. Murray Smith.

The cohesiveness of that Oilers dynasty reminded Edmonton sports fans of the atmosphere around the Eskimos in the 1950s. How lucky for hockey fans north of Red Deer that Sather had the foresight to look within his community for a solution. Gretzky's despair at the press conference announcing his trade to Los Angeles is evidence of the bonds between those Oilers.

Drake's record of 697 wins, 296 losses, and 37 ties was broken recently by Dave Adolph at the University of Saskatchewan. Upon retiring, Coach Adolph surprisingly revealed that Drake, his long time rival, had been his mentor. When Adolph needed help, Drake was always available. For Drake, the game and the people involved were bigger than rivalries or personal legacies.

None of the dozens of people interviewed for this book recall hoisting the championship cup as the most memorable moment from the season. The recollections always revolved around the team's achievements and the fun the players had. The thought of professional players in their twenties and thirties engaging in teen-like antics is amusing and is essential to building a team.

HUMOUR HELPS

Central to the 1950s Eskimos' way of having fun was to bet on almost anything they could set a wager on. Gambling was a regular pastime for many of the Edmonton players, though the outcome of games was not included. Still, a couple of the players in particular became incredibly imaginative in how to use ridiculous bets to get the competitive juices flowing. Mike Kmech, an all-star guard from Lamont, Alberta, recalled one day while waiting on the rainy tarmac of the airport how Norman Kwong and Jackie Parker amused everyone by staring at the window and betting on which raindrop would get to the bottom first. Another favourite for the two stars was betting on which elevator would get to the lobby first as the team waited to get to their rooms.

Gin rummy was a favourite way for Parker and Kwong to aggravate coaches and management, as rummy sometimes rivalled football for importance. The competitiveness of those card games was legendary. It wasn't uncommon for card games to go all night. In the morning, Coach Ivy would often send players to the rooms of gin rummy players who were late for the bus. It became so routine that the card players would purposely be late so that they could bet on which player Ivy would send. The antics surrounding the team created an atmosphere that made the workplace fun.

Player leadership was and remains a crucial piece in team building. There needs to be a leader in the group who has the resolve to do the right thing at the right time. The locker room and what goes on in there is beyond the reach of coaches. Organizations at all levels rely on clubhouse leaders' actions and work ethic to make the magic of a team happen. Great teams have great leaders, and often they are not the star players.

During the Eskimos dynasty, Coach Ivy gave the players a couple of days off after a win over a conference rival. After the euphoria of the announcement, rather bolting from the stadium, the players scrambled to their cars and went to a predetermined destination for a card game that lasted two days. The fellowship that Ivy and the Eskimos organization got from those joyous occasions outside of organized practices was crucial in winning championships. Coaches can set the table for greatness in several ways, and Ivy knew the leadership that emerged on those days off would pay dividends when football resumed. ·

Modern neuroscience has learned that laughter has considerable power in helping humans thrive. Closely related to laughter are joy and optimism. To test the power of laughter and positivity, how can one argue with holocaust survivor and psychologist Viktor Frankl, who believed that having purpose and laughter were the keys to him surviving the death camp at Auschwitz during WWII? .

While interned at Auschwitz, Frankl and his friend made a pact that they would get out someday, and they met daily to inspire each other through humour. They would joke about anything, including the guards' appearances. The two often reminisced about better times and vowed they would be freed eventually and find their purpose in life. Frankl believed that optimism and experiencing joy in our daily lives brings out the best in us, wherever we find ourselves. After his release from Auschwitz, he developed logotherapy, which was based on his experiences and ideas.

In any vocation, staff room/locker room morale is a good barometer of how the company, team, or department is doing. When Bob Dean became the principal at Victoria High School, one of his first moves was to inform the heads of all the departments to remove the coffee pots in their offices to force staff members to go to a central location for their coffee. There was some resistance to this, but as people began to mix with their colleagues, relationships were formed and the inner-city high school took on a new life. Dean learned he had allies in his fight to take back the hallways of his school and stop the bullying of staff and students.

As the only Asian kid on the block, Norman Kwong learned early in life that humour wasn't enough to survive. He had to punch first and follow up quickly with many more, as bullies were everywhere. Kwong's physical prowess earned him some elbow room. The future Stampeder and later Eskimo earned the respect of almost everyone in the community as a tremendous athlete with a wit to match. Luckily, Kwong found Coach Ivy and an organization that matched his personality.

Pop Ivy's pedigree was strong, having served on Bud Wilkinson's staff at Oklahoma. Between 1953 and 1957, the Sooners had an undefeated string of forty-seven games, a modern-day record for major college football. The Sooners were one of the greatest teams in football history, and their influence was far-reaching for many of the same reasons that the teams in this book are honoured. Ivy incorporated many Sooner practices into his coaching toolbox.

BROTHERS IN COMEDY—EDMONTON'S FULLBACKS

As good as Ivy was, he had a weakness that Kwong would exploit for the merriment of his teammates. Coach Ivy's expertise did not extend to telling players when their days with the Eskimos were over. Managers inherited the unfortunate task of cleaning out the lockers of cut players before they arrived. This highly impersonal way of releasing a player was an opening for one of Kwong's favourite pranks. Usually, he would pick a player, research his hometown, and prepare a travel itinerary for his return home. The prospect would arrive at his locker in the morning to find it empty except for a roadmap home with the best route and hotels highlighted along the way. Of course, the player was not cut, but the other players gave no hint of the prank.

One can only imagine the victim's suffering as he planned the call home to tell his loved ones the disappointing news of a shattered dream. The veterans would wait for the unfortunate player to arrive and observe as he gathered himself to leave. Only then would the laughter erupt, and his equipment would magically reappear. The prank worked often, but not usually with the veterans.

One time, an American who was having an exceptional camp arrived to find that his locker had been cleared out, and he assumed he had been cut. The team listened intently as Kwong's latest victim stormed into Ivy's office, demanding an explanation. The typically pious Ivy had had enough of Kwong's pranks. "Damn you, Kwong!" he hollered.

Kwong and Bright were equally highlighted in Ivy's double full-back system, as they had to block for each other as well as carry out their fakes with precision. If one of the fullbacks in the offence was not a complete player, the system would not work. The fact that both men were intensely competitive, and had terrific senses of humour made them the perfect complements for each other.

Johnny Bright was a highly sought-after speaker on the banquet circuit. On one occasion, he stated that Kwong's CFL record of seventy touchdowns was no big deal, as he only had seventy yards rushing. Bright elaborated that he did all the hard work getting the ball into scoring range, and Kwong got all the glory. Kwong replied that if Bright blocked as hard for him as he did for Bright, Kwong would have won the scoring and rushing title every year. Only players with a connection could joke about such things.

The attempt to develop a sense of humour and see things in a humorous light is some kind of a trick learned while mastering the art of living. – Viktor Frankl, *Man's Search for Meaning*

Somewhere in our evolution, teasing became an unusual way to demonstrate affection. The closer the bonds, the more personal it becomes. For outsiders, it's hard to imagine that people who like each other would talk like that. Teasing aims to soften our egos and make us more tolerant of one another. Locker rooms are notorious for this age-old practice. Teammates with fragile personalities learn to accept their "shortcomings" and soldier on. If a person is being teased, it's usually a signal that they are accepted and liked.

Johnny Bright's teammates knew the story of Wilbanks Smith's attack on him in 1951. Still, he realized that sometimes, confronting teammates with a bad memory or situation loosened them up. Bringing that hurt to the surface and making fun of it could aid healing. There was no place for playing the victim with men like Kwong or Bright. They knew all too well that learning and moving forward from negative experiences was the key to a good life. To highlight the spell that Kwong cast on this team, he would often creep up on Bright, grab him from behind, and shout, "Wilbanks!" Maybe Bright and Kwong "owned' Wilbanks by reducing him to a joke. It was like Kwong said, "Yes, we all come from different backgrounds and have all suffered in our ways, but we are brothers here and can be trusted."

Bright played the game in the harshest terms, and it took its toll. He understood the gridiron as he did life. Danger lurked everywhere, so he took it head-on. Offensive guard Mike Kmech remembered Bright returning to the huddle after getting tackled for a loss and asking his lineman to please get out of the way if they could not block anyone. Bright's approach to playing resulted in countless concussions, which became material for Kwong's comedic routine. As the *Edmonton Journal* reported on Jan. 16, 2005, "Bright used to hit so hard he would knock himself out so Normie would routinely flick the side of Bright's head with his fingertips and say, 'Goodnight Johnny.'"

In 1954, the Eskimos finished 11–3 during the regular season and won their first Grey Cup over Montreal. The play in CFL infamy is the famed Chuck Hunsinger fumble that Parker recovered and ran back close to eighty-five yards for a touchdown. The play is still somewhat controversial in Montreal, as it is felt that Chuck was trying to pass the ball as he fell. Ted Tully and Rollin Prather hit him high and low, forcing the fumble/incomplete pass that Parker recovered and ran for a TD. In the frequently run replay of that historical moment, you can see Bright trailing Parker the whole way. Legend has it that Kwong heard Bright yelling at Parker to lateral it to him so he could score. True or not, the story speaks to the camaraderie and fun surrounding that team.

Champions of the CFL – (L-R) Johnny Bright, Mo Lieberman, Normie Kwong and Jackie Parker

"ACCOUNTABILITY BREEDS RESPONSE-ABILITY." – STEPHEN R. COVEY

Fostering a belief in individuals that they must take responsibility for their actions is the foundation of any worthwhile endeavour involving adolescents or adults. Leaders can talk about accountability, but it is more important that it is modelled through hard work and attention to detail. When leaders make excuses, players will jump on the bandwagon.

Swiss psychologist Jean Piaget affected how a generation of educators viewed children's development. Piaget believed that at around age eleven, children began to separate from their parents into the larger community. Adolescents instinctively yet reluctantly seek order, as their racing hormones and changing bodies can be a potential problem. Hence, coaches embracing adult roles and effectively teaching solid values are invaluable in communities.

Connellan and his staff were committed to improving the community through their work with the Dinos. Connellan recruited accordingly and focused almost exclusively on southern Alberta. For men like Dennis Kadatz, Peter Connellan, and their mentor Murray Smith, the common goal was to apply the lessons learned through sport to improve their community. Holliday recalled Connellan's insistence that when their careers ended, they get involved in their community and help the next generation grow into adulthood. Connellan's message was clear and made an impact, as it was repeated by every Dino interviewed.

The Comets of Raymond mirrored the Dinos in player accountability. As Coach Ralph said, "We don't have a long list of rules, as the players aim to win a championship." On teams like Raymond or Connellan's, the players had a significant role in ensuring everyone had a common purpose. The day-to-day actions of the two teams are similar in many ways.

Teachers who coach understand the similarities between the classroom and coaching. Barbara Coloroso, a famed educator, had a similar approach to Connellan's. The three rules she gave her students on the first day of classes were simple: be on time, be prepared, and respect yourself and others. Confusion is reduced when the rules are simple. The last rule on Coloroso's list is what coaches do to encourage excellence. A lack of effort in Coloroso's classroom broke the third rule of respecting yourself and others. In team sports it is worse, as you are letting your teammates down. The key is to build a culture where excellence is the goal of the group.

HOLTZ AND CONNELLAN: "DO RIGHT"

In 1989, a few months after Lou Holtz won his national championship at Notre Dame, he addressed close to 1,500 coaches at a coaching clinic in Las Vegas. His helicopter to the roof of Bally's hotel was delayed thirty minutes, and the crowd was restless. Still, his reception was almost at the level of The Beatles at Shea Stadium. The audience scrambled over each other to get a picture of the coach of the year.

Holtz emphasized the role that discipline played in creating team culture. He had one rule: do right. Holtz explained that if he had to tell someone how to act, that player didn't belong in his program. The efficiency of Holtz's approach put the responsibility on the player to make correct decisions. The thoroughness of "do right" covered the classroom, players' personal lives, and football. Discipline was not a "sometimes" thing for men like Connellan and Holtz; it was an "all the time" thing.

Player leadership is evident in all exemplary programs. The engine that drives great teams like the Comets is the culture that the players embrace. They know the recipe for success, and their job is to execute it. The players' attitude is apparent as they begin warmups and move between drills. There is little overt supervision. Raymond players embrace maturity and responsibility.

Connellan left nothing to chance, including how his leaders were to act. His attention to detail was legendary, and his process regarding leadership was no different. Connellan's mentoring of Dinos leadership was a year-round proposition. In the summer, informal workouts occurred at numerous locations, led by "summer captains." Coaches could not be present in the summer as they would be violating the league's prescribed rules regarding the length of the season, but they had prepared their leaders to coach at those workouts.

In Connellan's words, "We had captains for everything: workout captains, summer captains, academic captains, unit captains, team captains." The goal was to develop the leadership skills of as many players as possible. The challenges, successes, and setbacks that leaders typically experience served them later in life when the stakes were much higher.

When Connellan started his leadership program, he found that January and February were good months to finish most of the work. At his weekly captain meetings, he asked them to generate the kinds of problems teams encountered and then worked together to find solutions. The sessions took place before classes began on weekdays and required sacrifice on the part of everyone. Players didn't get a captaincy for being a good player; they earned it. Connellan empowered his leaders and gave them the necessary skills to lead.

Thriving football communities teach the prerequisite values for having a purposeful life. As the founding father of the Southern Alberta Football League, Brian Dudley said many times in his interviews, "Those players are our community's future."

THE INFAMOUS COMETS VS. TEACHERS GAME

The coaches of good programs are well acquainted with purpose and optimism. Coupled with a strong dose of joy and humour, it makes for a team. During my interview with the Raymond founding fathers, Coach Gibb commanded his friend Brian Dudley to show me his finger and explain how he got it. As Brian put his hand on the table, my stomach turned as I saw what appeared to be something people would pay a toonie to see at the exhibition. The finger seemed to have a mind of its own, bent in several directions. Dudley laughingly explained that the injury to his finger occurred in a full-contact football game—without equipment—between the students and teachers. Lawyers would rub their hands in anticipation thinking of the fortunes to be made if such games were on the intramural schedule these days.

Dudley's injury was not the only one in that epic teacher-student battle. The teacher-librarian fractured his collarbone while making a tackle. Gibb and Dudley laughed as they recalled the librarian wore children's shoulder pads and demanded to be included. To make matters even funnier for the Raymond elders, it was his first play in the game, as the librarian was subbing for Gibb.

The legacy of that game was not the student victory but the stories that got bigger as the decades passed. The competitiveness of the Raymond sports community would never allow Gibb to forget that he'd had a chance to win the game for the teachers. Gibb, the running back, was tackled at the ten-yard line when the game ended. If he had scored, the teachers would have won and avenged the librarian's broken collarbone and Dudley's permanent disfigurement.

Gibb laughingly reminded everyone at the interview that his talents were underappreciated as a running back. He thought the teachers would have carried the day if he had handled the ball more often. The loss to the students on that fateful day nearly sixty years ago became part of that community's folklore.

THE DINOS' FRUSTRATED COMEDIANS

Every level of football demands slightly different things from its coaches. Coach Connellan of Calgary had a different challenge than a professional coach like Pop Ivy. Connellan had younger men struggling to find their game on and off the field. Connellan and his staff used humour to lighten the tension, as the players had unusually large expectations put on them. The Dinos lovingly referred to Connellan and his staff as frustrated comedians who made it a joy to practise, as they never knew what to expect.

The hijinks of Connellan in particular were unpredictable and potentially funny, yet respectful of his players. One former Dino remarked that what made those moments so memorable was that they were spontaneous and crucial to his concept of what a team should be. Dinos learned to laugh, and Connellan felt it was important they did.

The Dinos used the term "Connellan time," which meant that Connellan could be late, but the players could not be. It was inevitable that Coach Connellan would get caught up in some athletic department business at some point in the week. The time when the team was in limbo waiting for Connellan was often awkward. Still, it presented an opportunity for comedic leadership to emerge through players like Tony Spoletini. If coaches could be frustrated comedians, so could players.

Reminiscent of Normie Kwong in Edmonton, Spoletini was instrumental in creating a cohesive team. Once during "Connellan time," Spoletini took the lectern at the front of the auditorium and imitated the head coach and all his idiosyncrasies. Spoletini was notorious for getting laughs just by combing his hair like Connellan. Still, on that day, even comedian Jimmy Fallon would have been envious as he nailed his impersonation of the head Dino. Unfortunately for Spoletini, the players were not the only ones watching. Connellan was watching his performance from the shadows without his knowledge.

Blissfully unaware of Connellan's presence, Spoletini continued with his impassioned impersonation, much to the delight of the entire roster. A hush fell over the team as the coach made his presence known. As Connellan opened his notes, he could no longer contain himself and broke into laughter. According to eyewitnesses, the room erupted, and the effect on the team's camaraderie was immediate. Like Raymond's zany game between the staff and students, Spoletini and Connellan gave memories that lasted a lifetime.

One of Connellan's many gifts was being able to put people at ease. He easily shifted gears from being funny to serious when delivering his message. An example of the lengths to which Connellan would go to ensure his players were engaged would be to carry a water gun during film sessions and nail anyone dozing off. Although you will never find this technique in any teaching or coaching manual, it speaks loudly to the strange mix of playfulness and respect that

Connellan commanded. One can only marvel at the experience the Dinos enjoyed when one combines the comedic routines of players and coaches with championships.

A situation that can test the patience of any football coach is a play run incorrectly in practice. At some point during the season, the guards inevitably pull in opposite directions and collide behind the centre, which resembles a car crash in a silent film. When it happens, it is hard to contain the laughter at the astonishment of the guards as they hit each other. According to linebacker Keith Holliday, the team anxiously awaited the coach's response whenever something like that happened. If he laughed, the players would too, but if he did not, neither would they. Connellan's practice planning didn't allow for lapses in concentration. A repetition wasted in practice was gone forever. According to Spoletini, Connellan's unpredictability made the lighter moments more pleasurable.

TASTEFUL HIJINX

Rookie or initiation nights have become controversial lately, as skits and initiations can quickly get out of control. In some programs, the traditional rookie night has been eliminated. Because of their initiations, college fraternities are in the headlines yearly for injuries and even deaths. Connellan was proactive in his approach to initiation and had their rookie night under control in the 1980s. Players, coaches, trainers, and managers were all invited to rookie night, and the expectation was that nobody would feel disrespected. Many teams take the easy way out and cancel such affairs, but the Dinos were an exception, and they used the night to welcome newcomers to the team.

Before rookie night, Connellan communicated expectations to the captains and senior players. The consequences for players who broke the standards for a good skit were harsh. Dinos rookie nights made perfect sense, as they were fun yet honoured those in attendance. The message was clear: "We can have fun and have high expectations if everybody buys into our team's purpose." The dignity of everyone associated with the team was non-negotiable.

Connellan's team concept included protecting younger players from being matched with fourth-year players in hitting drills. His approach to recognizing the natural discrepancies in strengths between first-year students and seniors is not always present on teams. "I never wanted to see some big guy pounding on a little guy in practice, and the captains would usually step in to make sure it didn't happen."

The Spoletini cousins and their partner, Mike Palumbo, applied the Dinos' way to their wholesale and retail business. Employees and customers at Spolumbo's have responded to the Dinos' philosophy applied to business. Chris Lewis and Tony Spoletini related how Spolumbo's sausage-making began at 4:00 a.m. with the music cranked and. lots of laughter. After making the sausages, Lewis would get on the phone and make hundreds of calls throughout BC and Alberta, finding new retailers for them. The wholesale sausage-making began with only four people and was a happy, cohesive unit.

Eventually, Gerry Forbes from CJAY92 came onto the scene as a friend and started a comedic radio show called "Giuseppe the Delivery Guy," starring Tony Spoletini. Giuseppe became a colossal hit for CJAY92 and the sausage-making business. The four sausage makers would show up every morning and test run the Giuseppe sketches while CJAY92 cranked out the tunes.

It was easy to get up at 4:00 a.m. and start the day for young Chris Lewis. The imprint on Chris was permanent. It showed him he could have fun and win in business, just like Connellan's Dinos did on the field. Chris said, "It felt so good when you walked into an oil and gas boardroom with Spolumbo's catering, and the room would stand and cheer!"

During the covid-19 epidemic, the retail end of Spolumbo's suffered due to the lockdowns. With bills and staff to pay, finances were stretched to the limit. Spolumbo's was a longtime supporter of football in Calgary, and their generosity was recognized when the president of Calgary Minor Football implored the Calgary football family to support Spolumbo's. Tony was deeply touched by the support that Spolumbo's received from the community.

The key to the Dinos' success was having a solid philosophy and communicating it to the players. Connellan inundated his players with written material to connect his team with a particular way of thinking—the Dinos' way. The man who hired Peter was Dennis Kadatz, who played for Murray Smith with the Edmonton Huskies in the 1950s. All three men believed in communicating team values and practising them daily.

On game day, everyone had a clearly defined role. Everyone had a job to do, from the coaches in the booth to those on the sidelines. Not only did everybody have a job, they also knew why it was necessary to be done properly. The "why" behind the job helped motivate personnel to do their best.

The Dinos used a common language to clear up potentially missed messages between players and coaches. Connellan was a stickler for vocabulary. For example, a linebacker playing an outside technique had a specific name applied to it. That same name mimicked what the Dinos used to describe their opponent's linebacker technique. Many endeavours that involve high-pressure situations demand precise instructions. The military uses a process similar to Connellan's to ensure precision and effective action.

In examining the success of any perennial winner, people focus on the head coach and the playmakers. The head coach is usually the place to start, as he or she sets the tone. As former University of Calgary Sports Information Director Jack Neumann said, "It all started and ended with Peter." His mark was everywhere on the Dinos, including language.

BRICKLAYERS AND ARCHITECTS

Similarities between programs are easy to spot when you understand that a common philosophy can work in every team atmosphere. Like all sports, hockey is guilty of putting its star athletes on a pedestal. Dr. Smith recognized the folly of this, as star players would see the team bend to accommodate their wishes. Dr. Smith warned coaches and administrators against compromising the team's fundamental values in his work with Hockey Canada. Coaches who compromised their values for their stars and placed them on a pedestal were mistaken.

Teams need players in many roles. Sometimes the jobs aren't glamorous, but they're still necessary for team success. Soccer is no different from football in this regard. In 1998, an Italian national soccer team member famously mocked the French captain as a "bricklayer." Didier Deschamps shrugged off the criticism and replied that it was true—he was a bricklayer—but teams need bricklayers *and* architects. Deschamps's "water carrier" career included several European Cup Championships and a World Cup. He relished "carrying the water" for his more skilled teammates and cherished the nickname "Water Carrier" that teammate Eric Cantona gave to him.

The Dinos had an excellent feeder program in the St. Francis Browns. They were built along similar lines. Like Connellan, DeMan's conscience would not allow him to permit star players to break the rules. The values that made the St. Francis legacy were non-negotiable, and RB Chris Lewis learned that firsthand. DeMan called Lewis in after noticing that he had been acting up around the school. DeMan told Lewis he would not lie to a college coach if he inquired about his character. DeMan assured Lewis that he would speak honestly about his play on the field and his conduct around the school. Lewis recognized that it was in his best interests to change his attitude off the field, and he did.

With the Browns, it was about attitude and personality, Lewis recalled. "I came to understand this when I started managing people in business. High-skill, high-attitude guys were the best, but high-skill, low-attitude guys will eat your organization from the inside out. You cannot build teams with players that care more about stats than winning. Winning is tough." Lewis's consultancy business borrowed many ideas from DeMan and Connellan. The parallels between sports and how former Dinos and Browns conduct business are striking.

DeMan's understanding of adolescents was evident in his relationships with his players. Connellan was similar at the university level. Both programs brought order to the life of young men without being harsh or overbearing. Roles were defined and expectations were high regarding discipline, hard work, and teamwork. The high success rate that the Browns had at the college level was no accident.

One former University of Alberta Golden Bear, George Paleniuk, remarked that long after his playing days ended, he took notes on the Dinos' sideline, where the calm demeanour of everyone struck him. Trainers did their business, including filling water bottles and cleaning players' cleats as they got to the sideline. Coach Connellan seemed oblivious to the emotions around him, watching intently and making notes as the battle with their provincial rivals raged.

Spoletini corrected the recollections of the former Golden Bear close to forty years after that 1983 game in Edmonton. Regarding cleaning the cleats, "It wasn't the trainers but the players that were injured or not playing!" Spoletini said, his voice cracking. "It makes the hair stand up on the back of my neck when I think back to that Vanier Cup season in eighty-three and maybe one of the greatest Calgary high school running backs of all time [Elio Geremia] was cleaning the cleats of his teammates—doing whatever he could do to get us the win." In 1983, in his first year as head coach, Connellan successfully sold the concept of sacrifice that championship teams require.

DOGS AND DINOS BEFORE SELF

St. Francis had its share of great running backs dating back to the early 1960s, and Elio Geremia ranked right up there with the best. His decision to attend the University of Calgary was sweet music to the ears of Peter Connellan and former Browns on the team. Elio was the youngest of three brothers. In a *Calgary Herald* article by Steve Simmonds (Oct. 18, 1985), he referred to himself as a "hyper individual," even when he was small. "I was the guy running home from school when they walked." Older brothers Massimo and Bruno both played university football. Massimo was a running back at UBC, and Bruno was a defensive back at Calgary. In the words of Elio, "We've always been competitive. There was just one year between us all.

When one guy got a toy, everyone fought over it. Everyone wanted what the other guy had. Even in sports, the others wanted it when one guy won an award."

The competitiveness of Elio and his brothers was well suited to the Dinos. The commitment to the team that Coach DeMan instilled in his Browns made the Geremias' transition to the Dinos easy. Elio's remark after winning the Vanier but not winning the Hec Crighton as the most outstanding player in Canada best exemplifies his unselfish nature: "You can't drink out of the Crighton." The team spirit of those Dinos resembled and was directly linked to the Edmonton Huskies led by a young Dennis Kadatz twenty years earlier.

The source of Kadatz's magical "Huskies spirit" was no mystery to the national champion Huskies of the early 1960s. That spirit was inspired by Coach Murray Smith through his protégé, Kadatz. Kadatz also took sports psychology classes from Smith and played hockey for Drake at the U of A. The 1960s Huskies remain a tight group. Star lineman and future pro George Spanach recalls a team lacking in size but having an incredible will to win: "You were afraid to be the weak link on the team. You wanted to be worthy of the uniform."

Spanach's explanation for the Huskies' camaraderie was based on coach and player leadership and not wanting to let their teammates down. The use of film back then was limited because the cost of film was so prohibitive. Therefore, it was other players who were the most feared critics. According to Spanach, "Tony Rankel, the QB, would climb all over us. One time he said, and I was so embarrassed, 'Well, it looks like Spanach [an offensive lineman] made it through, but the RB didn't.' We all needed to prove to each other we belonged on that team."

Rankel and Bateman inspired and drove those Huskies teams. After Bob Bateman retired as a player in 1963, he continued with the Huskies in a director capacity. While in Vancouver to play the Meralomas in their drive to win a fourth national championship, the directors of the two clubs got together for refreshments the night before the game. A Meralomas director kept pestering Bateman to make a bet. A quick fight ensued in which Bateman came out sporting a black eye. Nothing was said the next day when Bateman showed up for breakfast. According to Spanach, no pep talk was necessary as the Huskies vowed revenge and achieved it with a victory over the hated Meralomas. The Meralomas had a long history of unsportsmanlike behaviour in the western finals against prairie teams who took great delight in beating them.

It is always a culture shock for players coming into the city from rural areas. Huskies alum Marv Roberts remembers being recruited from his central Alberta championship team in Ponoka by Norm Kimball and met in Edmonton by veteran lineman Bob Bateman. Roberts felt fortunate to have had Bateman take him under his wing in 1961, as Roberts was nervous about the move. The transition was challenging for Roberts, as he was intimidated by city life and the players from storied programs like Ross Sheppard and Strathcona. Fortunately, the team embraced the strapping young man from rural Alberta. Roberts's wedding party was evidence of the relationships made through junior football. It included Bob Bateman, Vic Justik, Ron Forwick, and Tony Rankel.

A cohesive unit will bring out the best in individuals who will go to great lengths to win a championship. Wally Cross, an *Edmonton Journal* reporter, wrote a column in November 1962 that examined the attraction of football.

> Last night, the Huskies trained as they have almost every other night since early August, only this night was lousier than others. A gloomy sky let loose with the occasional flurry of snowflakes, and the wind had obviously set itself on every iceberg between here and the north pole. At Kinsmen Park, where the Huskies mushed in the early hours of the evening, the weather veered from foul to wretched. They ran, slogged through the slush in a squish of cleats. They tackled and thumped each other in a grimy hog hollow, grunting figures in the dim light supplied by the odd 100-watt bulb. Oh, it looked like fun, friend.
>
> "Why do they do this kind of thing in this damn weather? They don't get paid for it. Do they find it

preferable to necking with a nice girl in a warm car?" "Desire is a corny word," said Hamilton. The players just got closer and closer as the season wore on. "Then he added the real reason. When you enjoy success as we have this fall, it's fun."

Another Huskies lineman, Dan Butcher, recalls his first training camp after moving from Two Hills in the late 1970s. Not having a place to live, Butcher sacked out in the backseat of his Plymouth Fury for the first week of camp. The 6'2", 255-pound lineman would wake up and go to a nearby gas station to wash and brush his teeth. As teammates got to know the shy seventeen-year-old farm boy, it became apparent that the future Edmonton Eskimo needed decent accommodation. Huskies head coach John Belmont came to the rescue and took him in until he could find a permanent place with a couple of his teammates. Now a proud Huskies Hall of Fame member, Dan is forever grateful for the thoughtfulness of teammates like Brent Pope, Ken Lang, and Coach Belmont.

A WINNING RECIPE DEMANDS THE BEST INGREDIENTS

Building a team at any level requires an equal mixture of talent and character. Pop Ivy's teams were an excellent laboratory for future scout Frank Morris. A Canadian Hall of Fame member and 1950s Eskimo, Frank Morris had a distinct advantage over most talent evaluators as he had played on six Grey Cup champion teams. He had witnessed talent and leadership and could recognize it in prospects. His genius at talent evaluation added seven more Grey Cup rings as the Eskimos' chief scout.

Former Winnipeg Blue Bombers scout George Paleniuk spent countless hours delving into the magic and methodology that Morris used to build the five-straight Green and Gold team of the 1980s. Morris had a simple formula for finding pro prospects. The two prerequisites for being a Morris pick were being a good fit for the locker room and a hard worker. A player liked and respected by his teammates is often characterized as "being good in the locker room." According to Paleniuk, Morris viewed his military experience as essential in helping him understand what a good team player looks like. Many scouts use the usual stats of height, weight, forty-yard dash, and so on to make their selections. This kind of scouting is quantifiable yet ineffective. In addition to the stopwatch, tape measure, and weight scale, Morris viewed the team trainer and equipment manager as essential resources who could speak to the character of a potential draft pick. He also had a habit of attending college practices to inquire about the best opponents in the league.

Some examples that show the shortcomings of tests in finding football players include arguably the greatest receiver in NFL history: Jerry Rice. His 4.71 second forty-yard dash time was well above the NFL combine average and he was seen by many as a questionable first-round pick.

Another receiver upon his retirement who set NFL records for most receptions in a career (819), most receiving yards in a career (13,089), and most TD receptions (100) was Steve Largent. Largent was easy to overlook mainly because of his stature (5'11", 187 pounds) and equally unimpressive speed in the forty-yard dash (4.8 seconds). Because of his lack of size and speed, Largent slipped to the fourth round of the NFL draft. Frank Morris believed the key to building a team went far beyond the "measurables," for you cannot quantify a player's heart and desire or their work ethic. Rice and Largent possessed the intangible characteristics that make good athletes great.

Morris had a bias toward football players who were athletic and competed in a variety of sports. CFL Hall of Famer and former Edmonton Wildcat Dave Fennell did not have the typical background for a defensive lineman. He doubled as an outstanding track athlete at the University of North Dakota. Other multi-sport Green and Gold linemen include Joe Worobec and Bill Stevenson in basketball and wrestling. Morris was a multi-sport athlete in his youth, excelling in football, hockey, and baseball. His Eskimos teammates, Rollie Miles and Johnny Bright, were also exceptional multi-sport athletes.

Morris watched players when the score was lopsided or the play was on the opposite side of the field for their "compete level." Players who gave up before the whistle blew or when the game was lopsided were not the kind of players he wanted. Another trick of Morris's was to go to the pregame to see players run routes and catch, as they may not get a chance in a game to get passes thrown to them. The members of those great Edmonton teams of the 1950s were lucky, as they had experienced the ultimate in pursuing and achieving excellence and knew how to spot it in others.

A GOOD RECIPE WORKS EVERYWHERE

John Belmont of Edmonton recalls Edmonton's Grey Cup teams of the 1950s with a mix of nostalgia and as an essential piece of his coaching education. After playing under coach Tommy Joe Coffey (CFL Hall of Famer and former Edmonton Eskimo) at Ross Sheppard High School in Edmonton, Belmont travelled south to Arizona State University in Tempe. John was a baseball and football player in his youth and tried his hand at baseball for the Sun Devils in Tempe.

In John's words, he discovered during his first year that he wasn't nearly as good a baseball player as he thought. The coaches, however, loved his work ethic and character and asked him to be the manager of the varsity team. Belmont's career at ASU was fortunate, as John was about to get an education in building a team from future Hall of Famer Bobby Winkles and football coach Frank Kush.

For over 200 years, the border between the USA and Canada has been uncontested. Trade has generally been mutually beneficial, with Canada's resources fueling the industries and manufacturing of the world's largest economy. The same sports are played in both nations, and coaching practices that work in Alberta are equally effective south of the border. Few Canadians have been fortunate to closely witness coaching brilliance in both nations in the same sports. John Belmont is one of the lucky ones.

The brilliance of those Winkles-led squads included coaching ASU alumni such as Reggie Jackson, Rick Monday, Sal Bando, and Larry Gura. In 1965 and 1969, Winkles was named NCAA Coach of the Year. *Sporting News* named "Coach Winks" Coach of the Year in 1965, 1967, and 1969. To top off his illustrious career, Winkles was inducted into the Collegiate Baseball Hall of Fame in 1997. The ASU baseball field was named in his honour, and he holds a storied place in American college baseball.

Winkles's version of team building in the desert was similar to the values used by the legendary teams much farther north. The Dinos, Browns, Huskies, Eskimos, and Comets of Alberta had much in common with the Sun Devils of Arizona. Sun Devils teams from the early 1960s still meet and use the same nicknames of yesteryear. Belmont's nickname was the White Rat, and his longtime friend Jim Merrick was the Hamster. When they encountered each other after several decades, those nicknames rolled off their tongues as quickly as "hello, how ya been?" Connections on good teams endure.

Frank Morris valued the opinions of team managers like John Belmont, as they saw the players and coaches when they were relaxed and away from prying eyes. How players treat others in an organization speaks loudly about their character. Tommy Lasorda of the Los Angeles Dodgers asked Belmont to discuss the character of Sun Devil prospect Rick Monday. The young baseball team manager from Edmonton, Alberta gave Lasorda the needed feedback. Kansas City made Monday the number one pick in the first MLB draft.

The New England Patriots and the New Orleans Saints are NFL teams that invest considerable time talking to trainers, college coaches, and opponents of potential draft picks. Like Morris's Eskimos, their records are always near the league's top. Team building requires choosing the right building blocks carefully.

WINKLES LIKE CONNELLAN

The discipline required of the players under Winkles was renowned. It was central to his goal of achieving unity and a common purpose. Sometimes coaches with high standards are seen as lacking in compassion or personality. Winkles was more than just a taskmaster. Like Connellan, he was also entertaining.

Winkles was an excellent public speaker with a great sense of humour. With the high standard he set for discipline, Winkles was emphatic in his belief that practices should be competitive and fun. Like Bright and the Lancers, Winkles challenged his players through playful bets and seldom paid up if he lost or collected when he won. He kept his players loose but always on task. The similarities between successful programs on both sides of the border are striking and follow similar themes.

Belmont's coaching career is still going strong fifty-eight years after those early years in Arizona. John's career demands attention, as his dedication to football may be unprecedented. Belmont's teams were a reflection of Winkles's and Kush's coaching principles. The uniforms and equipment Belmont ordered were of the highest quality, and players were expected to treat their uniforms with respect. Like Belmont's Arizona State mentors, fundamentals and conditioning were the foundations of his teams. Belmont's one-liners and folk wisdom have made an impression on several generations, including members of the same families.

Unlike Jim Ralph, Lou Holtz, and Peter Connellan, Coach Winkles had a long list of rules. ASU's players and managers never walked but ran on the field. Winkles felt strongly about wearing suits and ties whenever the team represented the university. Sal Bando, the team captain, learned the consequences of not abiding by the dress code. Like the Huskies' Bob Bateman, with Winkles, nobody was above the law.

ASU teams were much like the Green and Gold in their obsession with games of chance. Winkles allowed gambling, but the amounts wagered were limited to a certain amount. Before a regional playoff in Utah, the guys ran out of chips and pop while playing cards. Bando ran across the street to remedy the situation, although he failed to put on the mandatory jacket and tie. The next day when the umpire read the lineup card, he noticed that his name was not on it.

Belmont recalls Bando returning to the bench a "whiter shade of pale." Winkles had spotted Bando the night before on his chip run, and exceptions for superstars were not forthcoming. Dr. Murray Smith would have been proud. For men like Smith, pride in appearance and the discipline to follow team guidelines mattered. Fortunately, the Sun

Devils won even without their captain. They went on to the national championships, for which Bando was in the lineup.

Winkles's benching of team captain Sal Bando in a playoff game was extraordinary in that the values that built that team would not be compromised regardless of a player's stature. Situations like Bando's are a real litmus test for a coach, as penalizing a star player hurts the team's competitiveness. For that reason, star players are often given a free pass for violations of team protocols, which has the unfortunate consequence of cracking the team's foundation.

A rapidly changing society heavily influenced the early 1960s in North America. WWII, the Korean War, and the emerging civil rights battles in America influenced the men who led teams in that decade. Men in uniform understand the benefits of teamwork and how a uniform helps to build camaraderie and spirit. A dress code coupled with discipline crossed economic and racial lines. People were accustomed to men and women in uniform and understood a uniform's purpose.

WORKS IN BUSINESS TOO

Cam Stewart was a defensive end on John Belmont's team in the mid-1970s and enjoyed a stellar career with an American-based world leader in office furniture. When asked to reflect on his team building techniques in business, it became apparent there was a crossover to sports. Alberta's elite football teams indulged in much of the same processes. Like Spolumbo's, humour, purpose, and optimism were the values Stewart used to build a winning team.

Stewart pointed out that stars exist in business, and he had to deal with their transgressions just as Winkles and Kadatz had to deal with their captains' transgressions. Stewart stated, "Dealing with broken rules by your stars was a great opportunity to show everyone what you stand for. Goals were set not to meet dollar targets but to bring out the best in people." One can easily see Coach DeMan nodding in agreement with Stewart's notion that the correct process produces the best results—better people.

Stewart's philosophy was different from what many in business use to guide their management of employees. He believed managers should accentuate people's strengths and soften the effect of things they cannot do. "To create a team, you then take everyone's strengths and play off each other, but everyone must abide by a set of core values." Corporate leadership acknowledged that Stewart's team consistently achieved its goals. They made up for what the Western Canada branch lacked in superstars with a solid, team-first philosophy. Stewart maintained that having a westerner in charge of the western USA and Western Canada who understood the culture west of Winnipeg and the Mississippi was important. Western business people appreciated open and honest communication.

As Coach Connellan inundated his players with the Dinos' way in written and verbal ways, Stewart did the same with his international team of employees. Conflicts between clients and sales associates were sorted out in face-to-face conversations where dignity and respect mattered. Connellan and Stewart both used the term "dignity" freely and frequently.

EVERYONE MATTERS

Jack Neumann, the Dinos' sports information director, believed Peter Connellan's gift lay in his ability to make everyone feel a part of the team's success. "It wasn't uncommon for him to come in on the day of the game and tell me to crank it up a notch as it was a big game today." The Dinos' philosophy and mantra were central to Jack's relationship with the team. "TEAM—together everyone achieves more."

In whatever community, plumbers are indispensable. Without plumbers and plumbing, there would not be any clean, fresh water, and diseases like cholera would ravage communities. In the same way, the equipment manager and trainers have a crucial role on a football team. Without them, the team is in trouble. On many teams, support staff operate quietly in the background. Mike Newans, the equipment manager of those 1980s Dinos, worked differently.

Holliday and Spoletini had big smiles when describing Mike Newans's role in the team's success. Newans loved music, and the early 1980s were exciting as new genres emerged. The players raised money to put a stereo in the locker room and put Mike in charge of picking the music. As Spoletini put it, "He introduced us to ska, surf music, punk, and reggae. We loved it, as it was so much fun. We just respected the guy and the pride he had in his work."

The Dinos took pride in their uniforms, and Newans took the Dinos' appearance on game day to the degree of a bride's mother on her daughter's wedding day. Their uniforms were folded the same way every game day and delivered by Newans with a game face that rivalled those of the players. For him, the uniform symbolized the Dinos' commitment to excellence. Many Dinos commented on Newans's intensity in fulfilling his role and saw him as an essential leader.

A humorous side role that Newans offered the Dinos, which turned out to be a great team builder, was when he started doing haircuts for the players. It began with a couple of guys getting surfer cuts, and eventually, it spread. When word got out that Newans was doing haircuts on a particular day, the lineups were long. The Dinos loved and respected him as the Huskies twenty years earlier had adored their trainer, Monty Ford.

TRAINERS HAVE THE PULSE

Monty Ford is a well-recognized name in Edmonton's sporting history. Monty was the trainer for the Edmonton Mercury hockey team that won the gold medal at the 1952 Olympics. Evidence of Ford's popularity was the 125 guys who showed up at his 75th birthday party. In Terry Jones's *Edmonton Sun* column on June 19, 2012, Ford is described as a colourful character who was the source of many fond memories.

George Spanach recalled, "If you thought you were hurt and Monty came out there to look at you and you weren't hurt that bad, he'd call you a 'wildcat.' You'd get back up and get in there." Ford wouldn't tolerate players being hurt to escape a difficult situation.

Hugh McColl Jr., a star linebacker, recollected that Monty unconditionally defended his guys regarding penalties. Some Huskies felt his vigorous attacks on referees might have cost them more than a few penalty flags. When Monty Ford's name is mentioned, the faces of veteran Huskies who knew him break into big smiles.

FRANKL NAILED IT

Monty Ford was the Western Canadian exemplar of Frankl's three fundamentals of a good life. He would have identified with the notion proposed by country singer Reba McEntire that everyone needs three bones: a wishbone, a funny bone, and a backbone. McEntire's recipe for success mimics Viktor Frankl's view that humour, optimism, and purpose are essential for a good life. For teams to work, they need people like Monty Ford.

All teams have a sense of purpose, but some have it more than others. The Comets, Huskies, Eskimos, Browns, and Dinos had the right formula for producing a sense of team. The process that fed success included players like Kwong, Bright, Spoletini, and Kachman of the Huskies and support staff like Newans and Ford. Such individuals brought the necessary work ethic, fun, and optimism to reduce the load.

As a young boy watching the Huskies, I loved seeing their reaction to Monty Ford at the end of the bench, stomping the ground with one foot and clapping his hands in rhythm. I was troubled by the man's timing, as he always clapped and stomped when things weren't going well. Later, I realized that Ford knew that enthusiasm was most important when the team needed it most. When Ford clapped and stomped, the Huskies always responded with a spirited cheer and began clapping. Monty wouldn't let his boys quit—ever.

The third ingredient that was impossible to ignore was the optimism or belief that they would put the best version of themselves on the field every week, whatever the odds. Leadership from various sources creates and nurtures that positivity and optimism. The leaders who led these teams were solution based when problems arose and looked forward to the chance to compete.

The competitive aspect of football is well known and appreciated by players and their fans. What isn't well known is the mental and physical resolution required to play the game. The competitive edge is honed and encouraged in hours and hours of practice. During these practices, the hand-to-hand combat of tackling, blocking, and shedding is drilled repeatedly. Some players are naturally courageous, but others learn through hundreds of repetitions.

Players must carry out their jobs precisely and consistently. A missed block or assignment can result in a severe injury or defeat. As in all contact sports, the best teams have a "team first" mentality that understands the whole is greater than the parts. There is an old saying in football that a game will be decided in one or two plays. The problem is that you never know when those plays will happen. Players and coaches on successful teams understand and practise the often-used cliché of being all-in on every play.

Speaking to a reporter, the late Mike Leach, NCAA football coach and larger-than-life personality, once compared commitment in a football game to breakfast. He believed the referee's investment did not approach that of the players and coaches. "It's a little like breakfast; you eat ham and eggs. As coaches and players, we're like the ham. You see, the chicken's involved, but the pig's committed. We're like the pig, and refs are like the chicken. They're involved, but everything we have rides on this." The honesty required to be their best is the commitment coaches speak of and look for in their athletes. Leach meant no disrespect to fans or officials, as they are an essential aspect of the game experience, but that is where the difference lies.

-4-

GO WEST YOUNG MAN! FOOTBALL'S MAGIC IN ASSIMILATING NEWCOMERS

Alberta is loaded. In 2022, Alberta's provincial GDP was twice the national average. The "Wild Rose" province owes its prosperity to its geography, institutions, and Albertans of all shapes, sizes, and colours. We were all drawn to this province for its abundant resources. If you go back far enough, those resources included mastodons and, later, agricultural, forestry, and petroleum products, which the world desperately needs. Before giving ourselves a big pat on the back, we must understand that Albertans did not make the oil. It took millions of years before humans or dinosaurs for the region to accumulate the decaying algae, plants, and tiny organisms that give us oil. The Western Interior Seaway cut North America in two as it stretched south from the Arctic Ocean to the Gulf of Mexico. The boundaries of the sea were the Appalachians in the east and the Rockies in the west.

Contrary to popular belief, dinosaurs were not involved in the production of Alberta crude, as they came well after the sediments from the sea had covered the gazillions of small, decaying creatures. This seaway existed when the planet had a much warmer climate. The fossil evidence can still be seen in the imprint of sea creatures on rocks throughout the Prairies and on the eastern slope of the Rockies.

In certain areas, the oilsands came to the earth's surface. First Nations communities utilized the oily sand for various purposes, including oiling their canoes and leather clothing. The area near Fort McMurray was famous for oil reaching the surface. Research at the University of Alberta was started in the 1920s to process the oil from the sands in which it was locked. It wasn't until the 1970s that an economical extraction method was completed that could make usable products.

An outstanding debt is owed to the Western Interior Seaway and all those creatures that ended up being the hydrogen and carbon mix that made Alberta the destination of humans from the four corners of the planet. The discovery of natural gas in the Turner Valley in the first three decades of the twentieth century vaulted Alberta into the largest gas-producing region in Canada. Subsequent oil and gas discoveries in the Leduc area eventually gave Alberta tremendous economic clout nationally and internationally. Until 1951, Saskatchewan had a larger population than Alberta, and Alberta was one of the poorer provinces in Canada. As Alberta's status in Confederation grew, so did the awareness of the region's unique political, social, and economic structures.

Alberta's relatively recent arrival on the world economic stage attracted attention from international investors in energy, forestry, and agriculture. Western Canada's role in Confederation was changing, and many in Alberta demanded a more significant say in how the federal government spent their resource revenues. The rise of fringe political parties that wanted to separate from Canada made many in central Canada curious about Alberta.

BERTON AND THE PRAIRIES

Authors with large audiences nationwide also gave Alberta's history attention. Pierre Berton was one such writer. He had roots in the Yukon and BC but enjoyed tremendous success after he relocated to Toronto. A strong nationalist, Berton wrote many books about the origins of Canadian culture and its British roots in Ontario that spread across the continent with the railroad. Fortunately, Berton grew to appreciate that Western Canada was more than an extension of central Canadian culture and values.

The loyalists who fled the USA during the American Revolution greatly impacted the institutions that led to Confederation in 1867. Still, Western Canada had a much more complicated history than many Canadians would like to believe. We in the West took a much different path to the present than many in Central Canada believed.

The spirit of optimism was strong in the early West. People came to Alberta and the Prairies looking for a better life and were willing to endure intense hardships. Optimism is embedded in the spirit of Western Canada. How else could one look out on a frozen, snow-covered tundra in February and start planning for a spring seeding of crops and vegetables?

Readers generally regarded Pierre Berton as providing lively, entertaining, and accurate books about Canadian history. Berton's books on the building of the railroads and the battle at Vimy Ridge paint a picture of how Canada came to be. His book *The Promised Land* was an interesting take on Western Canada.

During the research and writing of *The Promised Land,* Berton's thinking on Western Canada changed. The more he delved into the rich history of the land west of the Great Lakes, he was struck by how culturally different it was from Canada's other regions. Far from simply being a land of English-speaking settlers from Ontario, Berton felt it was one of the most diverse regions on the planet. Western Canadians had long known they were culturally different from Central and Eastern Canada, but hearing it from a nationally recognized figure was nice.

Westerners with ancestral roots located elsewhere also understood that they were not the first people to settle in the area that used to be the Western Interior Seaway. The melting of the last ice age close to 13,000 years ago heralded the arrival of First Nations peoples and culture into North America. For 12,000 years, unique and diverse First Nations communities thrived on the North American continent.

The arrival of Europeans changed the landscape. Diseases brought from Europe devastated First Nations peoples across the Americas by about 1870. Near the turn of the century, the increased activities of farmers and ranchers were instrumental in ending the way of life for thousands of First Nations people. The most notable evidence of their decline was Louis Riel's rebellion, which was easily put down by a small force. Over one hundred years later, First Nations have emerged as a political and economic force on the Prairies.

The long-held perception in Canada was that English-speaking settlers settled in the West. Although English-speaking settlers were Alberta's largest group, this assumption ignored the First Nations and Metis cultures and German, Ukrainian, Swedish, Norwegian, American, Icelandic, Scottish, Irish, Russian, Black, Japanese, Polish, and Chinese contributions of the early twentieth century. The reality of immigration to the West was that Germans and Scandinavians were accepted, and Ukrainians and Slavs were tolerated. The groups that faced the worst discrimination were Blacks, Japanese, and Chinese, who were repeatedly blocked from entering the country. The internment of Ukrainians and Japanese during WWI and WWII are examples of the unequal treatment of newly arrived Canadians.

SPORTS AS A BRIDGE

Sports play a role in bridging the many cultures that can divide communities. Lois Hole, former lieutenant governor of Alberta, often stated that public schools were crucial in a culturally diverse society, as they bring people from different backgrounds together and teach them that their similarities far outweigh their differences. Hole felt that working through and discussing projects in the classroom sets the stage for building an inclusive community. By extension, the sports offered in these schools further encourages the integration of non-English-speaking students who suffer from discrimination.

The history of sports in the public school system may have been one of the ways the lieutenant governor described how people from diverse backgrounds could become better acquainted. Lois Hole's children, Bill and Jim, excelled at football with the University of Alberta in the late 1970s and are remembered as good teammates and people.

Throughout her term as lieutenant governor, Lois Hole stressed the need for understanding and compassion in a community. The interplay between the Hole brothers and their teammates may have contributed to their mother's thesis that diversity and inclusion can be nurtured through educational institutions and athletics. The actions of individuals/families speak louder than words. In this regard, the philanthropy of the Hole family has left a deep mark on the Edmonton community. Lois Hole would easily accept Sun Tzu's thoughts on building an army and adapt them to her views on community: "When one treats people with benevolence, justice, and righteousness and reposes confidence in them, the army will be united in mind and all will be happy to serve their leaders."

Benevolence, justice, and righteousness are the end goals of most communities that value democratic ideals. Sports teams that model these values are essential in communities as people often look to such teams for inspiration. Successful coaches and programs attract even more attention, none more so than a sport Hall of Fame.

Bill Parcells gave his NFL Hall of Fame induction speech in August 2013. The colourful coach did not back away from controversy. Like many induction speeches, Parcells emphasized the importance of building community within a team. As he said, he didn't get there alone. Parcells said that having a common purpose and being accountable to one another were the keys to building community.

Inclusion on any successful team is about a person's willingness to sacrifice for the team's benefit. For Parcells, sports teams should function as a meritocracy where the best players play regardless of skin colour, sexuality, or religious affiliation. For Parcells, the proof that the NFL had taken considerable strides in achieving a true meritocracy was the number of people of colour present at his induction as fans and inductees—past and present.

Parcells overwhelmed his audience with his message of hope, which revolved around personal accountability. Athletes earned inclusion in the world's finest football league by taking responsibility for their performance. The following is an excerpt from Parcell's speech.

> Now, talent aside, we know it's the football business, but the only prerequisite for acceptance into that locker room is you've got to be willing to contribute to the greater good, and if you are willing to do that, you are readily accepted. If you're not, you're pretty much quickly rejected. Now we've got all kinds in this place. We've got white, we've got Black, we've got Latin, we've got Asian, we've got Samoans, we've got Tongans, we've got Native Americans. Ladies and gentlemen, I played and coached with them all, and the only thing that made any difference is, are you willing to help? And if you are, come on in. If you're not, get the heck out of here.

> Now, there are many exit doors in pro football, and by exit doors, I mean vehicles that organizations, players, or coaches could use to incite the public that it wasn't their fault that the team performed poorly. But Monday, about 5:00 in the afternoon after we've all watched those films, very seldom are any of those exit doors taken, because accountability is at a premium in guys like this. It's at a premium.

Parcells's message in 2013 aligns closely with Alberta's traditionally conservative nature over the last seventy years. Alberta's recent arrival on the international economic stage has attracted people for myriad reasons, but financial opportunities are usually at the forefront. The push to immigrate from a country might be for economic or social reasons, but the country they are contemplating moving to must have a few good reasons to pull people to it. Alberta's few good reasons include economic prosperity in a community that has rewarded hard work.

In his international bestseller, *Sapiens*, Yuval Noah Harari describes humans as a "two-legged movable feast." The feast that brought so many people to Alberta is still based on resources. Harari's credentials are impressive, but his revelation that humans are greedy for resources is hardly news to anyone whose ancestors recently immigrated to Alberta.

The pull of immigration to the province was Alberta's rich resource base, which supplied basic sustenance and gave Albertans leisure to pursue social and sporting activities. Through these activities and commerce, recent groups of immigrants have shown more settled residents they are, as Parcells described, "willing to help."

Oxford graduate Niall Ferguson wrote a book called *Civilization* that sums up Western civilization's ascendancy because of six values: competition, science, property, modern medicine, consumerism, and work ethic. Nowhere in Ferguson's work does he attribute the West's success to biological factors such as race or gender. Ferguson saw the spread of those six values as good for humanity, as their adoption has increased longevity and material happiness.

FOOTBALL AND INCLUSION IN ALBERTA

Football evolved to its present form in the late 1800s. The British influence of rugby had a prominent role in football formation, and the games still have several shared characteristics. Rugby football in Canada resisted American adaptations for a time, but eventually, stoppages and restarts of plays became the norm on the Prairies. The forward pass also found its way to Alberta, but interestingly, the Rocky Mountains proved to be a barrier to the game's spread to the West Coast. British Columbians were reluctant to embrace changes to the game of rugby. The "Britishness" of our western neighbours has diminished, but in the 1930s cars still drove on the left side of the road.

Sports were played well before Europeans came to Western Canada. One game that women played mostly was called two-ball. The game was played on a field around a half mile long with poles on either end which two balls secured by a leather thong had to be wrapped around. The two balls could be advanced only by a metre-long stick held by the players. The players needed help to move the ball forward with their feet or hands.

Sports played a significant role in breaking down negative racial stereotypes and encouraging diversity in Alberta. One need look no further than the fullback tandem of Kwong and Bright for a story to back Parcells's claim that sports can facilitate inclusion in a community. In the first half of the twentieth century, Alberta was demographically very different from what it is today, with an overwhelming majority of the citizens being of European ethnicity.

The lives of ordinary citizens are often good sources for inspiration. Kwong Lim Yew (Norman Lim Kwong) was born to a Chinese immigrant family in Calgary, Alberta on October 24, 1929. His father, Charles Lim Kwong, immigrated to Canada in 1907 and was forced to pay a head tax. After 1903, the tax approached $500, which was what a labourer could expect to earn in two years. The tax was an attempt to prevent Chinese immigration, but in reality, the tax prevented wives from uniting with their husbands and children from uniting with their fathers.

The Chinese Exclusion Act of 1923 came close to stopping immigration from China. The Canadian government repealed the act in 1948, and immigration was made more inclusive. The political atmosphere at that time was full of anti-Asian rhetoric, making life difficult for young Asians like Kwong.

When Kwong's father immigrated to Canada, he soon found the degree of racism in British Columbia intolerable. Upon his arrival in Calgary, Charles and his wife, Lily, noted that although racism existed, it was endurable, so he started the Riverside Cash and Carry store in the city centre.

As a youngster, Kwong hid his skates in the garage so his parents would not know what he was doing with his spare time. This aversion to sports was hardly unique to the Chinese community, as many newcomers to Alberta found a bounty of riches there for the taking. They thought young people should earn money, get better grades, and not waste time playing games. Upon his retirement as lieutenant governor, Kwong said he hoped that Chinese Canadian parents would embrace sporting activities such as football and hockey for the social benefits they offer to youngsters. For Kwong, a child's education is more complicated than memorization and learning facts. People's skill sets can be sharpened through the give and take of play.

During Kwong's lifetime, Alberta dramatically improved in the area of inclusion. As Kwong said in a Feb. 4, 1989 *Edmonton Journal* article, "It is an entirely new world. Nobody remembers except us old-timers." A year before Kwong played in the 1948 Grey Cup with the Stampeders, the immigration ban (Exclusion Act) on Chinese people was lifted in Canada. Between 1923 and 1947, less than one hundred Chinese people immigrated to Canada.

The CFL's outstanding Canadian in 1955 and 1956 and the outstanding Canadian athlete in 1956, laughingly recalled how his mother, Lily, found out about his football prowess by seeing his picture in the paper during his high school years at Western Canada High School. The emergence of a Chinese Canadian football star in Calgary was newsworthy. The Chinese community in Calgary had trouble finding work due to discrimination, so the luxury of athletic pursuits was not high on the Kwongs' priority list.

The assimilation of Chinese Canadians was difficult. Kwong recalled how banks or department stores did not accept his sister's job applications. Many Chinese people anglicized their last names to pass screening processes that excluded Asians. One Chinese Canadian running back from Strathcona High School, Adrian Marr, remembered how his father, an accountant trained at UBC, changed his surname from Mar to the Scottish equivalent of Marr. After several rejections as Quintin Mar, he was offered an interview and received a job at Porta-Test Engineering as Quintin Marr.

Upon entering Western Canada High School, Kwong excelled at football and went on to play for the Calgary Stampeders from 1948 to 1950. One rumour regarding the hometown boy's trade to Edmonton was him seeking traditional Chinese medicine for an ankle sprain rather than having surgery, as the team expected. The Stampeders' medical team was perturbed at being ignored by Kwong and might have hastened his trade to Edmonton. Edmonton was eager to sign Kwong, as the Stampeders' Grey Cup victory in 1948 had greatly embarrassed the province's capital. The competition between Alberta's two major urban centres was as fierce then as it is now.

The healthy competition between Edmonton and Calgary has had many interesting side effects, including the Eskimos' formation in response to the Stampeders' Grey Cup win in 1948. Edmonton business people had enough of the press that Calgary was getting and raised sufficient funds to have a professional team to compete for the Grey Cup. The availability of an athlete like Kwong from the championship team was an opportunity that Eskimos manager Annis Stukus could not pass up.

Kwong's prowess on the field deserved the highest praise. He was inducted into the Canadian Football Hall of Fame, where he was recognized as one of the best players in CFL history. The "China Clipper" played for the Eskimos from 1951 until his retirement in 1960. He was a quick, powerful runner who blocked equally well. One of the longest-standing CFL records was Kwong's 1,437 yards rushing by a Canadian in the 1956 season. Jon Cornish finally broke the record over fifty years later. However, Cornish had three more games in his season than Kwong did.

Kwong would be the first to admit that his achievements are a testament to his teammates and the Eskimos organization. Kwong occupied a special place in the hearts of his teammates, and his affection for them was evident at one of the last functions he hosted as lieutenant governor. Kwong's sense of gratitude was clear that evening as he acknowledged his teammates and their wives as instrumental in breaking down barriers and bringing him so much joy.

Bright and Kwong played similar roles in Coach Ivy's offence. Ivy adapted the double fullback system from the previous coach's (Darrell) Royal) split-T. Both fullbacks were remarkable athletes and shared similar personalities in that both were unusually good at making people feel at ease. Their unselfishness was infectious.

A YOUNG SCOTSMAN AND THE ESKS

The Eskimos' success helped ease the transition of one young man in his move across the Atlantic to Canada. Brian Dickinson remembers the Eskimos' impact on him as an immigrant from Edinburgh, Scotland. To help sell the young Dickinson on moving to Canada, his father told him that the professional team there had won three consecutive Grey Cups. Brian's cousin had immigrated a couple of years earlier, so in the fall of 1957, he took Brian to his first football game at Clarke Stadium. They sat with the famed Knothole Gang in the north end zone. According to Dickinson, the game was a complete mystery to him, as he didn't know what was going on at Clarke Stadium with nothing but "bums and elbows coming at him."

Years later, the future special teams and running backs coach of the Eskimos reflected on how his coaches with the Jenner Pontiacs were retired Eskimos he had watched in 1957. They were like gods for Dickinson, and he was excited to play for them. The transplanted young Scotsman adapted quickly to the strange North American version of rugby and found himself in grade eleven, playing with the Edmonton Wildcats.

Dickinson's conversion to football was complete and dominated his young adult life. Immediately after school, Brian would help George Kingston coach the junior team at Queen Elizabeth High School from 3:30–5:30, then grab a bite before going to the Wildcats practice. Brian excelled at football, and the respect he earned on the field enabled him to meet people who remained his friends for life.

The Wildcats in the 1960s included many first- and second-generation Canadians. They formed a bond in their uniqueness, with football allowing them to integrate into the community. Coaches and peers who spoke English were a bridge into this new world for new Canadians.

The Wildcats of the 1960s were highly competitive and may have been the best team in Canada if not for their crosstown rivals, the Edmonton Huskies. The Wildcats' place in Edmonton sports history is assured, as they have their share of national championships and alumni who have done great things in the community. Civic leaders like Jack Rutherford and Mayor Bill Smith were proud former Wildcats.

Football's impact on Dickinson made it hard for him to turn his back on a game that gave him so much. He graduated as a player from junior football into Edmonton's coaching ranks as an assistant coach with the Wildcats. During his tenure, Brian coached and became friends with many of the Eskimos from the 1950s.

Due to their excessive snoring, Bright and Dickinson were destined to be roommates on Wildcats road trips, as no one wanted to share a room with them. Dickinson was amazed after hearing of the racism that Miles and Bright had to endure that they could put it behind them and be such strong contributors to their new community. Dickinson remembered Bright describing how determined Drake's opponents were not to let a Black man beat them.

The ferocity of racist opponents had a terrible effect on Bright's teammates. Bright recalled that his offensive line would eventually give up in the face of such fanaticism. Even Bright would cringe at his stories of the abuse he received from opposing fans, coaches, and players.

Bright was sensitive to the racism in Alberta, but over time the acceptance of the community and his teammates overwhelmed the negativity he encountered.

Black American teammates; Miles, Bright, and Walker earned the opportunity to find purpose in their lives after football by educating young people. Not only did they find teaching jobs, but their students adored them. Art Walker's tragic drowning death cut short his remarkable legacy working with Edmonton's inner-city youth.

Dickinson asserted that Bright, Walker, and Miles changed Edmonton for the better and that the community's maturation in racial matters gave the American football stars a sense of optimism of better days to come. Evidence of Bright, Miles, and Walker's commitment to the city of Edmonton through volunteerism was everywhere. The positive two-way relationship between Edmonton and its star players during the 1950s had a lasting effect on Canada.

BRIGHT, MILES, AND WALKER'S LEGACY

By freely giving one's time, a volunteer meets at least two principles necessary for a good life: purpose and optimism. The hours spent volunteering by Walker, Miles, and Bright had the unintended consequence of familiarizing a predominantly white community with African Americans and seeing them as significant contributors to Edmonton's well-being.

The renaming of Jasper Place Bowl to Johnny Bright Sports Park and the Southside Athletic Grounds to Rollie Miles Athletic Park are tributes to the efforts of those men in making Edmonton a better community. The countless hours Bright, Miles, and Walker offered to the youth of Edmonton made them feel appreciated and even loved. One could only imagine the thrill Bright or Miles felt as they walked into a gymnasium or onto a field. They had earned deep respect as champions and men who cared deeply about young people in Edmonton. Although Alberta was not a utopia for inclusivity in the 1950s, the province had improved a lot over a decade.

During one late-night conversation between Bright and Dickinson, Bright confided that he was hurt that the Eskimos had never asked him to coach. Dr. Gary Smith picked up on Bright's disappointment at being overlooked by the Eskimos, which motivated Smith to publish a dissertation on racism in the CFL. It is challenging to find the flaws in Bright's football resume.

Dr. Smith felt Bright's tactical innovations in the late 1950s and early 1960s were cutting edge. Smith recalls Bright running no-huddle and hurry-up offences long before they became fashionable south of the border. The Lancers of Bonnie Doon also emptied the backfield and ran six receivers long before Doug Flutie and the Argonauts made it commonplace.

The question remains: why was Bright denied the chance to coach Edmonton's beloved Eskimos? Bright had demonstrated at the high school and junior levels that he had the commitment and the ability to build the relationships that coaching required. With all his playing and coaching credentials, many felt Bright deserved a chance to coach professionally.

It was difficult for the Miles family when they first arrived in Edmonton. Rollie and his wife, Dr. Marianne Miles, had difficulty renting accommodation. An Eskimos director showed them an apartment above a retail store. Marianne found it unacceptable and wondered if a White American would have been offered less-than-average accommodation. The Miles family quickly found more suitable living arrangements, but questions remained.

Dr. Miles remembered Edmonton in the 1950s as much different than today's community. Racial slurs were common and seemed accepted by most people in the community. Within the White community, slander was commonplace and divided people based on nationality or culture. Even in the Catholic Church, racial lines existed, as the Miles family waited for Whites to accept communion before they went up.

Bright and Miles came to Alberta looking for opportunity and found it in education. Miles used his education and his personality to achieve great things for the Edmonton Catholic School District. After Miles's athletic career ended, he taught at St. Joseph's High School and later became the supervisor for athletics in the Catholic system. Miles's presence at sporting and district events was always memorable, partly due to his wonderful smile.

Miles's arrival in Edmonton was not the usual signing of a top prospect. *Edmonton Journal* reporter Don Fleming notified the Eskimos when Rollie Miles arrived in Edmonton with a professional baseball team from Regina. Miles was introduced to the Eskimos' Al Anderson, who immediately signed him to a contract to play football. Miles earned the MVP award in 1951, 1952, and 1953. Heisman Trophy winner Billy Vessels played on the 1953 team with Miles, yet Miles won the team award. Billy Vessels, the former Oklahoma Sooner star, won the CFL MVP award as a consolation.

Darrell Royal, the Eskimos' coach in 1953 and long-time Texas Longhorn coach, called Miles the most outstanding athlete he had ever coached. Royal coached several NFL Hall of Famers, the most notable being running back Earl Campbell of the Houston Oilers.

Royal's well-founded praise for Miles as an athlete was seen in a game against the Winnipeg Blue Bombers when Miles was the last man standing, as the first- and second-string QBs were injured during the game. One Winnipeg reporter said it was like the "Bombers were chasing a ghost." After the game, Winnipeg fans stood and cheered Miles for the fantastic exhibition he put on that day. The respect paid to Miles was even more remarkable because Edmonton won the game. A Winnipeg reporter remarked, "Winnipeg football fans are not particularly noted for their charitable treatment of Blue Bomber opponents. The ovation they gave little Rollie Miles was all the more convincing because of it." In addition to Coach Royal's endorsement, Ray Willsey, an Edmonton Eskimos player who became the head coach at the University of California and assistant coach with the Oakland Raiders, called Miles the best player he ever saw.

MILES, DEAN, AND A YOUNG JEWISH BOY

Upon his induction into the Canadian Football Hall of Fame, Miles thanked his teammates and coaches but saved a special thank-you for a local businessman named Henry Singer. Singer's advice, which Miles was grateful for, was to stay in Edmonton, as it would be mutually beneficial for both parties. Miles was significant in Singer's Jewish community, often at bar mitzvahs and other events. Coach Dean's star kicker at Victoria High School, Jack Schwartzberg, remembers how Miles was a role model and hero for young men in the Jewish community.

Schwartzberg credits athletics as a key component in his transition to a new culture and country, similar to Calgary's Normie Kwong. Jack Schwartzberg, a future placekicker and star basketball player with Bob Dean's Victoria Composite team, had Polish parents of Jewish descent who survived the Holocaust in Nazi concentration camps. Schwartzberg's mother, Ida, worked at two camps, the last being Ludwigstove, where she made munitions for the Germans. Jack's father, David, was a slave labourer at several camps: Sakenheim in 1940, Annendora in 1941, Brande Breslau in 1942,

Tarnowitz in 1943, and Markstad from 1944 to 1945. It was on the march to Buchenwald in 1945 when the Americans liberated him. Jack's parents met in Munich after the war.

David and Ida Schwartzberg (Jack's parents) were among the 250,000 Jews put in displaced persons camps, which the UN operated throughout Germany, Austria, and Italy. These camps were holding areas to help relocate people around the world. David and Ida found their way to Bolivia in 1948, as Bolivia was one of the few South American countries that would take Jews.

The decimation of Europe and the displaced persons caused by WWII are well known. Canada's role in accepting refugees like the Schwartzbergs greatly benefited our country's economic and social fabric. However, before the war, the world, including Canada, was reluctant to admit Jewish refugees into their countries. In 1938, a ship called St. Louis sailed from Hamburg to Havana with 907 Jews on board. The craft and its passengers, including Canadian ones, were denied permission to land at ports in the United States and in Canada. The consequences for the passengers were tragic, as the ship returned to Germany, and nearly all its passengers were killed in Auschwitz.

Jack Schwartzberg's journey to Edmonton and, ultimately, to Bob Dean's Victoria football team began in the terrible conditions of postwar Europe. Europe's infrastructure and agricultural land had largely been destroyed. General Eisenhower informed Congress that tens of millions of Europeans were within weeks of starvation. Roads and bridges were often impassable, and necessary funds came in the Marshall Plan passed by Congress, which freed billions of dollars to help rebuild Europe.

When the Schwartzbergs arrived in Bolivia, they found themselves in the middle of a revolution that promised to extend the vote to females, redistribute land to peasants, and give the regions the right to control their natural resources. The USA found itself on the revolutionaries' side against the Bolivian oligarchy. By 1949, the revolutionaries had control of over half the country, including the Schwartzbergs' new residence of Cochabamba.

"I was a survivor, and my parents were survivors," Jack said. "When I was growing up, there was fighting in the streets every week. I was in jail when I was eight—nothing scared me." Jack was incarcerated because he dropped a boulder through the window of a police car that was driving by. The policeman caught him and put him in a holding cell with other criminals. When the policeman called his dad to explain what Jack had done, his father told the officer to keep him there for the day to teach him a lesson.

Jack and his buddies were safe playing soccer, as the revolutionaries and government troops were not interested in shooting children. Soccer was a religion in Bolivia, and when Jack had the chance to watch the national team in his hometown, he sneaked into the stadium and stayed all day watching his heroes. On the way home, his buddies warned him he was in trouble with his parents. Kidnapping was a regular occurrence in Bolivia, and his parents feared that Jack had been abducted. Jack said his father made his rear end look "like the stripes on the American flag," but he learned a lesson. Shortly after that, the family immigrated to Edmonton, and Jack's father opened a butcher shop called Schwartzberg's Kosher Meat Market on 124th Street and Jasper Avenue.

Holocaust survivors Ida and David Schwartzberg with son Jack

Jack's love of sports grew as Edmonton offered the young fellow a chance to make friends and have fun. He remembers playing basketball, running to the corner store, and returning with chocolate milk to the Wesley United Church for his pals Larry Dufresne, Ken Van Loon, John Belmont, and John Hennessy. His friends were older, and the chocolate milk was the price of admission into those pickup games. In grade ten, Jack had the unique distinction of winning the city championship in junior and senior basketball for Victoria High School on the same day. During Jack's time at Victoria, he was involved in one of the great upsets in Alberta sports history.

Victoria High School won the provincial championships over the famed 60–0 Raymond Comets led by Tim Tollestrup and Allan Williams the following year. Jack remembers playing full-court press against them as Vic's coach, John Baker, felt they would get soundly beaten if they played zone. In the game's final minute, Jack came from behind the Raymond guard late, dove, and forced a turnover that resulted in a basket, finalizing the win. That turnover reminded Jack of something his father taught him that helped him survive in the concentration camps during the war: "If they pick your pocket, you pick theirs."

The young Schwartzberg desperately wanted a souvenir from that monumental upset in front of a packed house at the U of A. He could not get the game ball from the referees or the net, as the university raised the hoops, but Jack proudly owns the scoresheet from that day, which he picked "from the pocket" of the score table.

The actions of Tim Tollestrup's father after one of the greatest upsets in the history of Alberta high school sports deserve attention. Tim and Wally were Canadian basketball stars in the 1960s and 1970s. Some credit the Tollestrups with helping initiate the current Canadian invasion of the NBA. As Jack described the scene, a large man approached him after the game and said, "Number twenty-four?"

"Yes, sir," Jack replied.

"You sure upset the applecart today!" the man said. "My name is Mr. Tollestrup, and you played a phenomenal game. I want to congratulate you myself." Close to sixty years later, Jack is still amazed by the strength and grace of a man who could remain so dignified after his proud community lost such a heartbreaking game.

The hardwood at the University of Alberta played out a drama larger than the upset of one of the greatest basketball teams in Alberta history. The story of Jack Schwartzberg is a testimony to the value of sports in a community. Schwartzberg became a multi-sport athlete at the University of Alberta and a successful businessman. According to Schwartzberg, he owes more than just a few guys a thank-you.

Schwartzberg's story is what former Lieutenant Governor Lois Hole saw as the value of public institutions in integrating communities. The son of Holocaust survivors was befriended by a group of Christian boys who pulled the young Jewish guy to their basketball games at the United Church in West Edmonton. The minister needed a soprano, so he recruited Schwartzberg to sing "O Holy Night" in the church choir. Schwartzberg was happy to oblige the minister, as he spent so much time playing basketball there. Bob Dean recognized the heart and competitive fire in Schwartzberg and recruited him in grade twelve to play for the city championship team alongside other refugees from postwar Europe. From his birthplace in Munich to revolutionary Bolivia and finally to Edmonton, Schwartzberg found happiness, purpose, and friends through sports.

Later in life as a basketball referee, Schwartzberg remembered a valuable lesson from Dean: you should always stand tall and look comfortable in any environment. The fearlessness of Schwartzberg's parents and Coach Dean resonated strongly with Schwartzberg, and he learned never to flinch under challenging situations as a referee. Old coaches teaching the right things have a lasting legacy.

Schwartzberg used his knowledge as a referee to climb to the pinnacle of officiating on the international stage. Still, it was there that he was reacquainted with the reality of antisemitism. In 1983, Edmonton hosted the Universiade Games, and Schwartzberg was selected to be a table official, responsible for checking the score, fouls, timeouts, and so on. Schwartzberg witnessed how an Egyptian referee was to be paired with an Israeli for a game that Schwartzberg would be working the table for. The Egyptian declared that he could not be partnered with an Israeli. This was not due to his beliefs but for reasons of safety. FIFA was unhappy with the Egyptian referee's stance, and he apologized but said that he would be killed on his return to Egypt if he was seen working with an Israeli.

The Universiade held in 1983 cannot be mentioned without talking about the gold medal that Canada won in men's basketball. Before ten thousand fans at Edmonton's "Butterdome," Canada shocked the USA team in the semi-finals, 85–77. The American team included two future Hall of Famers, Charles Barkley and Karl Malone. Also on the American squad were several future NBAers, including Raptors Ed Pinkney and Kevin Willis. Sitting in the stands watching were another couple of Hall of Famers, Bill Russell and Bobby Knight. Hats off to Jack Donahue and his players for giving Edmonton such wonderful memories.

Support from spouses is necessary for most meaningful endeavours, and referees' families are no different. Schwartzberg recalls how his wife, Rowena, had no problem with him spending his Friday and Saturday nights officiating at the University of Alberta. A side benefit for Rowena was the domestic tranquillity she enjoyed as Schwartzberg took the children with him. Their kids loved going to the games and even tore out the bottom of their popcorn tubs to amplify their booing of their refereeing father's unwanted calls. Their children, Stevie and Daryl, loved those games as much as their mother enjoyed the quiet time at home.

Stevie's life was taken from him too early at age thirty-five by a rare disease called familial dysautonomia. Years earlier, the graduating class applauded and stood En masse when Stevie's name was announced at the Ross Sheppard graduation ceremony. It was a testament to his spirit, which personified his Hebrew name, Simcha, which translates to "joy and happiness."

Schwartzberg, the street soccer player from revolutionary Bolivia, learned for survival reasons that words are powerful weapons in diffusing difficult situations. One night while refereeing a game in Edmonton, Don Horwood, the hometown coach, followed Schwartzberg up and down the sidelines, constantly complaining.

Finally, Schwartzberg said, "I like Friday nights, Don, because I get some peace as my wife doesn't have me at her beck and call, but unfortunately, you've become my second wife." The three-time national championship coach smiled and then left Schwartzberg alone.

Seven-time national champion coach Ken Shields at the University of Victoria also was on the receiving end of Schwartzberg's rapier-like wit. The future Order of Canada recipient dissected one of Schwartzberg's calls by saying, "A good ref wouldn't make a call like that." Dumbfounded, Schwartzberg took a couple of steps and then replied, "A good coach wouldn't say something like that." Shields smiled, and through his silence gave Schwartzberg his due. Coach Dean would have been proud of his manager/kicker's grit in standing his ground in the face of the Hall of Fame coach's bullying.

Victorious Golden Bears win Vanier Cup in 1972. (L-R) Larry Tibble
– QB, Clarence Kachman – Alum, Jack Schwartzberg – Rec/Pk

THE ARRIVAL OF DISPLACED PERSONS FROM EUROPE

The Victoria Composite football team of the mid-1960s showcased the advantages of opening one's doors to refugees. In addition to Schwartzberg, Victoria had the Jereniuk brothers and George Paleniuk. Their families had also experienced the horrors of enslavement by the Nazis. Bo Jereniuk was the QB and George Paleniuk was a two-way lineman with the team. Both players came from displaced persons camps in Austria. Loaded onto converted cattle cars in Halifax, the boys and their families eventually found a new beginning in Edmonton.

Jereniuk's father was a tailor in the work camp, and he found similar work in Edmonton. Jereniuk remembers, like other recent immigrant families, the reluctance of his parents to endorse athletics as a pastime for their children. Paleniuk also faced similar difficulties with his parents, who viewed it as a waste of valuable time better used in academic pursuits or on the job making money.

Jereniuk's parents, Otto and Vera, were interned in a camp that supplied armaments for Germany's war effort. Jereniuk remembered his father's story of how the Allies bombed the factory they worked in to stop production. The roof collapsed during the bombardment. When freed, Otto discovered that the men who had sought shelter with him were dead. Otto went outside, brushed himself off, and thanked God for sparing his life. The near miss convinced Jereniuk's father that he was spared that day for a higher purpose, and he lived his remaining days accordingly.

Otto Jereniuk earned favours in the camp by using his skills to appease the camp guards. One way he could get extra food or cigarettes was to use his sewing skills to repair the camp guards' uniforms. Otto's abilities with a needle and thread were substantial, and when Vera agreed to marry him in 1946, he fashioned a beautiful wedding dress for her made from a white silk parachute. The newlyweds left the church and returned to the displaced persons camp in a limousine that an Eastern European entrepreneur had converted from a hearse. In 1948, the newlyweds were put on a boat and landed in Halifax.

ST. FRANCIS HIGH SCHOOL AND THE
POSTWAR WAVE FROM ITALY

Another group that found refuge in Alberta after WWII were the Italians, mainly from the southern region of Italy known as Calabria. The St. Francis Browns are famous for the many players of Italian descent who played there. The root of immigration from Italy was the economic decimation the region suffered during WWII. Immigration from Italy to Canada became extremely popular in the postwar era, as many former prisoners of war immigrated back to Canada. Metropolitan areas across Canada embraced the strong work ethic and family orientation the Italians brought with them to Canada.

Gary DeMan was the first coach in St. Francis's history. The school was built in 1961 and inherited a large group of first- and second-generation immigrants from Italy, Poland, and Ukraine. In his first year, DeMan took a junior team to the city championships, where he lost to the perennial champions, St. Mary's. DeMan recalls that the Italian community made up close to half the school population for several years, but few of those students played football. Football was a tough sell for recently arrived Canadians as many viewed leisure sports as a luxury they could not afford.

The year 1970 was a watershed for DeMan and the Browns. The city championship they won that year over Ernest Manning, led by Peter Connellan, highlighted the kicking of Frank Santacroce. Tony Spoletini said that the game-winning kick made headlines in the kicker's hometown in Italy, as someone forwarded Santacroce's picture and the accompanying article. The prestige and attention that young Santacroce's kick made in Italy found its way back to Calgary's Italian community.

The repercussions were huge for football in Calgary. DeMan noticed the influx of community support almost immediately. The following year, the floodgates opened and DeMan had access to the massive Italian community in his school. It took years for DeMan to build his program, but the school did not realize its potential until football assimilated the school's large Italian community.

Many families left their mark at St. Francis but none more significantly than the Forzanis. Few families in Canada's sporting and business history have reached the heights of the Forzanis. The passing of John in 2014 at age sixty-seven revealed the impact that the family had on their hometown of Calgary. Not only were the Forzanis great football players, they were equally adept at business and later as philanthropists. In his eulogy for John Forzani, Ken King, president and CEO of the Calgary Flames, said, "This is a beautiful man—a beautiful person. Very few people fall into this category. The city lost a friend of the community. A friend of the city. He just wanted to do nice, important, valuable things for the benefit of those people and the community" (*Calgary Herald*, Oct. 31, 2014).

Joe Forzani's decision to play football at St. Mary's changed the trajectory of his younger brothers. With the opening of St. Francis on the north side, John Forzani was united through football with Coach DeMan. Younger brother Tom followed John but was a basketball player until his senior year when he played football. Utah State also benefited from the Forzanis' love of football, as all three boys went south of the border to play after high school. At one point, the Stampeders had all three Forzanis on their roster.

Tony Spoletini's parents were first-generation Canadians who, according to Spoletini, did not know anything about sports. "My relatives wrote to whatever country would take them. I have cousins in Australia and the USA and you went to wherever they would take you. I have cousins playing footy, cricket, rugby, whatever. I think what helped us be good at St. Francis was seeing how hard our parents worked to put cleats on our feet." Spoletini's recollections are repeatedly shared by first- and second-generation Canadians and put an exclamation mark on how vital sports were for integrating into the community.

TWO PEAS IN A POD—FORTINI AND KWONG

Current St. Francis principal Luigi Fortini recalls keeping his playing for the Browns a secret from his parents. According to Fortini, his father and most first-generation Canadians did not understand the game and felt that their sons should be working, not playing. In one game, Luigi suffered a broken collarbone, and his sister drove him to the Holy Cross Hospital, where his father was employed. Fortunately, his father wasn't working that night, but he found out two days later from the doctor that his son broke his clavicle playing football. Luigi laughingly recalled that he expected to have his other clavicle broken by his irate father, but nothing transpired. The Fortinis produced another Brown, as Luigi's son continued the tradition, playing at St. Francis and later with the Dinos.

After school, most of Luigi's elementary school friends were bussed home to the community of North Haven, and he soon found himself alone at Browns practices, shagging balls for the kickers and generally being a nuisance. After a couple of weeks, Coach DeMan approached the young Fortini, introduced himself, asked him his name, then asked if he would like to be the water boy. Luigi recalls travelling with the team on the bus and being immersed in Browns football. DeMan quickly became Luigi's mentor and motivated him to get into education. Nearing the end of his career at St. Francis, Fortini recognizes that although his style differed from DeMan's, they both agreed that their job was to "do what is best for the student." If discipline is required, administer it. If a pat on the back is needed, give it.

Future Principal Luigi Fortini at St.Francis as a young equipment manager between two of his big buddies.

NEW CANADIANS FITTING IN

Tony Spoletini remembers his awkwardness as a young Italian at the lunch table in elementary school. The third-, fourth-, and fifth-generation Canadians would pull out their peanut butter and jelly sandwiches, and the Italian kids would pull out torpedo buns loaded with mortadella, provolone, and prosciutto. The Italian kids felt so self-conscious that Tony and his friends often agreed to trade their mamas' creations for the North American sandwich. When the critical thinking parts of their adolescent brains started to develop in junior high, the Italians knew they were getting ripped off. The days of ravioli in a can are now over as the growing popularity of the Italian centre in Edmonton and restaurants like Spolumbo's in Calgary forever changed Alberta's palate.

It is unnecessary for someone to come from another region in North America or to cross the ocean to face difficulties fitting into a community. George Spanach remembers moving to Edmonton from the Coal Branch area south of Hinton and attending Ross Sheppard High School. Shep was a football powerhouse in the early 1960s with a larger population than Spanach's hometown of Mercoal. George did not play football until his grade twelve year, and he had no idea what equipment was needed or how to put it on. His friends told him all he needed was a sweater. "I brought the nicest sweater I had," he said. "It was a red Orlon sweater inappropriate for football, but my friends found me another one, got me dressed, and away we went." Indeed, away he went to three national championships with the Huskies and later to the Eskimos and Alouettes to play professionally.

Proud grandsons, Mathew and Brendan,
wearing George Spanach's championship jackets

The Alberta of the last seventy years has seen economic growth and prosperity, but challenges remain. In the next seventy years, Alberta's economy will probably transform, and individuals and strong public institutions will be key. Institutions are the key to transforming economies and communities. The institution of sports cannot be ignored. Kwong, Miles, Bright, Getty, Lougheed, Dean, and the Forzanis attribute much of their success to athletics, particularly football. These men embraced the opportunities Alberta offered and embraced the responsibility that came with their success.

The most significant resource in the game of football is the volunteers, who invest a vast amount of time and energy. Football remains a great way to assimilate newcomers into a community that benefits from the diversity that recent arrivals can offer. The weight of that responsibility is difficult for coaches and volunteers, but the rewards are immeasurable. School coaches are volunteers who are not paid and rarely receive time off for the time spent coaching.

-5-

TEAMS AND COMMUNITIES IN SYNC

"My sons won Grey Cups, but the best times were playing with their friends at Raymond. It's a special thing when you put on a Comet uniform for the first time and look in the mirror. It's been placed on you to carry on the tradition." – Jim Ralph

The southern Alberta towns of Raymond, Cardston, Magrath, and Stirling were founded at the turn of the last century by Latter-Day Saints or, as they were called then, "Mormons." The early pioneers migrated north from Utah and Idaho looking for land and the freedom to practise a controversial aspect of their faith, polygamy. The land they pioneered required canals for irrigation, and their industriousness was well suited for the task. Agriculture soon flourished as water was diverted to the semi-arid fields.

The Knight Sugar factory was an essential industry in the early years, attracting many Japanese immigrants and formerly interned Japanese Canadians. All communities are unique in some way, but the towns south of Lethbridge near the USA border are distinct from similar-sized towns in the rest of the province. The geography of Alberta south of Calgary is breathtaking and lends itself well to large ranches with isolated pockets of irrigated land that produce abundant crops. Sugar beets and corn were, until recently, a southern Alberta specialty.

Recreational activities initially revolved around agriculturally based themes. Raymond is proud to have held the first Stampede in Alberta in 1902, predating the now legendary Calgary Stampede by ten years. Southern Alberta has maintained a rich tradition in rodeo to this day.

Alberta's interior plains are divided into three main areas: grassland, parkland, and boreal forest. Raymond sits in the grasslands of the south. The isolation the area enjoys has allowed it to develop a faith-based culture that is distant and distinct from the province's two major metropolitan areas of the region, Edmonton and Calgary. Ranches and irrigated agricultural land drew subsequent pioneers to the area, but the Latter-Day Saints' cultural and religious imprint was deep.

Nothing will get a person up in the morning like a good rivalry. The intensity of the Raymond community spirit may be due in part to events over one hundred years ago when the LDS Church leadership in Salt Lake, Utah had a tough decision. They had to decide on the location of the first temple outside of the United States. The temple site is enormously beneficial to an area, as the temple serves several significant purposes. Temples are essential for the Church for many reasons including marriage, which binds men and women and their families for eternity in the worship of Jesus Christ.

After much deliberation, in 1914/1915, Church leadership decreed that Cardston, not Raymond, would be the site of the temple. Raymond's disappointment at the decision must have been profound, as the community went so far as to artificially construct Temple Hill in anticipation of getting chosen. Some, including Blair Bennett, feel that the choice of Cardston as the site helped strengthen a sense of community in both centres and intensified their rivalry. In Bennett's words, the "rivalry is fierce."

The competitive spirit in southern Alberta unites communities and also glorifies the victors who bring home the laurels. Ribbons for participation mean nothing to the elders of southern Alberta.

They crave trophies. In the words of legendary football and basketball coach Bob Gibb, "The best athletes come from families that go way back. Champions come from families that were champions before. We believe in this town. We want to live with champions, and we want to be around the jacket!"

If Gibb was not clear enough as to the Raymond ethos, you can go to the town website, which describes the municipality in five ways: "Where Champions Live," "Where Champions Play," "Where Champions Grow," "Where Champions Create," and "Where Champions Make History."

IT WASN'T EASY IN THE BEGINNING

Raymond has a rich and storied legacy as a hotbed for basketball. Some of the finest teams ever to run the hardwood in Alberta practised and played in the LDS gymnasium. Raymond basketball was a well-established tradition in Alberta, and for a long time any sports that detracted from the game that put Raymond on the map were discouraged. The thinking was that a town the size of Raymond could not afford to have a variety of sports competing for a small number of athletes. Rather than have several mediocre teams, Raymond opted to excel at basketball.

An outsider in the mid-1960s challenged the sports hierarchy in Raymond. When Brian Dudley moved to Raymond from Fort Macleod, he was approached by a man from Calgary named Evans to start a football league in southern Alberta. Dudley was sold and felt it would be a great idea but ran into a roadblock in Coach Bob Gibb of the basketball Comets, who was dead set against the introduction of football. It was no accident that an outsider brought football to Raymond.

Gibb's objections were well-founded as football was rough, required many coaches, and the boys had no experience with the game. Another consideration was that Raymond's tiny population barely had enough athletes to field a basketball team, let alone the thirty players that a football roster would require. Eventually, Gibb surrendered to Dudley's passion and even agreed to help coach the football team. The two became friends and have had a deep mutual respect lasting nearly sixty years.

Dudley's impact on Raymond went far beyond mentoring young men through football. Bob Gibb pointed out that Dudley was responsible for starting a theatre arts group for Raymond that still puts on musicals and plays. In addition to his commitment to the fine arts, Dudley sat on the town council and was instrumental in building a new stadium for the community.

Legendary Raymond coach Brian Dudley with former
Comet and CFL Hall of Famer Lloyd Fairbanks

AN OUTSIDER ON ATHLETICS IN SOUTHERN ALBERTA

Dr. Blair Bennett, a proud football alumnus of Bonnie Doon in Edmonton, was always fascinated by the athletic success of Raymond. Because of his LDS background, Bennett was well acquainted with southern Alberta and wondered how Raymond could beat the Lancers of Bonnie Doon, led by Johnny Bright. As a teen he couldn't help but question why the taller, bigger students walking the halls of Bonnie Doon were not playing basketball or football. Bennett quickly learned that city kids had many more options and took advantage of them. Not everyone in Alberta shared the LDS obsession with basketball and football. Raymond's culture within southern Alberta was and remains difficult to replicate in large metropolitan areas. Only some children grow up wanting to be Bonnie Doon Lancers in southeast Edmonton, but in Raymond, almost all kids dream of becoming Comets.

Jim Ralph believes coaches, school administrators, peers, parents, teachers, and the community are all involved to a far greater extent than in other communities, and he may be right. Finding adults willing to work with young people is always easy in Raymond. When Dudley decided to pass the coaching reins to Mark Beazer, the Comets did not miss a beat when they transitioned to twelve-man football.

Women's athletics have kept pace with the men in southern Alberta communities. Just a few miles down the road from Raymond sits the town of Magrath, which also has a strong sporting legacy and has won a few provincial basketball titles. In 2022 the Magrath women's basketball team battled Raymond to the last minute, only to lose in the Provincial 4A final. Raymond's women's rugby team are perennial champions every spring and arguably more consistent than the men in bringing home the hardware. Women's sports have prospered in southern Alberta. Many provincial title banners hang in the Cardston, Raymond, and Magrath gymnasiums. The athletic success of these small communities speak to the importance that the Latter-Day Saints place on mentoring and investing in their young people.

Ex-Lancer Blair Bennett was a Quorum of the Seventy member responsible for thousands of Latter-Day Saints across Western Canada and Northwestern USA. His job allowed him to travel and accumulate a suitcase full of stories. One important stop in southern Alberta for Bennett was Magrath, which is located 15 minutes from Raymond. The demographics of Magrath are similar to Raymond's, and it has a rich tradition in athletics.

After Magrath High School won the provincial men's basketball title several years ago, Bennett seized an opportunity to meet with the team's captain. He told him a more significant challenge would be presented to him as a leader when he started his mission. The skills required by leaders are complicated, and men like Bennett knew that values were at the heart of a leader's competency. Bennett believed being a team leader did not end when the final whistle blew. He approached the captain of the Magrath team after the end-of-the-year banquet and reminded him that his responsibility to his teammates did not end with basketball. The more important role the captain would play, Bennett informed him, was to convince his team members to do their two years of mission work upon graduation. Much to Bennett's delight, the captain contacted him two years later and said the last of the team had just left for his mission. Athletics plays an essential role in the life of LDS, and sometimes the overlapping schedules of spiritual obligations and sports events produce an interesting dilemma for church leaders.

One year during his tenure on the Council of the Seventy, Bennett scheduled a stake meeting in Magrath at the end of March. Without realizing it, Bennett had put the meeting smack dab into the middle of the provincial playoffs. When the weekend of the meeting arrived, an anxious-looking man reminded Blair that the meeting was at the same time as the provincial final and that the Magrath Zeniths would probably be in it. Blair could not cancel the meeting, as religion trumps basketball, but he did move the meeting an hour earlier and remove the lunch break so everybody could get to the game. Bennett laughingly recalled his honest mistake and the compromise that avoided a crisis in faith.

A similar dilemma faced the prophet of the church several years earlier. "The BYU game will not be over for at least two hours. In fact, I've cut my talk a little short so that you—not I, but you—can watch it." President Hinkley drew many laughs from the congregation for his comments. Brigham Young University was named after the second prophet of the Church and has a rich athletic tradition. Brigham Young succeeded Joseph Smith as the leader of the Church and was the great-grandfather of Hall of Fame QB Steve Young.

TRADITION AND COMMUNITY

Vibrant communities with rich traditions, like those in southern Alberta, worry about becoming complacent. As Jack Neumann rhetorically asked me at our last meeting, "How long does it take to build a house, and how long does it take to tear it down? Alumni of successful programs are reluctant to let go of the values that made them strong."

Chris Lewis addressed succession with the retirement of DeMan and how the Browns' values continued with an alum named Joe Stambene taking the helm. Every coach today at St. Francis is a graduate who played under Stambene. The discipline demanded at St. Francis endures. As Lewis says, "Helmets stay on the whole game. Nobody sits down unless they are talking to a coach. Discipline, discipline, discipline! Young coaches with no affiliation with that central value lack the consistency in how they manage the team, call a game, and everything else."

One former Dino recalled how Dinos graduates were instrumental in saving and reviving Atom football in Calgary. The Atom coaches needed to catch up on the big picture and were more concerned with winning games than letting youngsters experience a great game. "Some coaches were blitzing all the time, and one kid would run the ball all the time," Spoletini recalled. The league stepped in under the guidance of League President Greg Peterson (former BYU Cougar and CFLer) and mandated several rule changes to facilitate a better experience. It became illegal to cover the centre, so he could make his snap. Only two carries are allowed for an athlete in a five-play series, each team starts at the forty-yard line and gets five plays and then the other team gets their turn, and in every series, there must be one pass. The net result of these changes was increased enjoyment, and enrollments increased accordingly.

Former Stampeders Greg Peterson and Spoletini played a decisive role in getting all the outlying minor football leagues together on several issues. A considerable outcome of that collaboration was the improvement of Shouldice Park. Note that the Calgary Minor

Football Association is a volunteer organization with no paid members. Peterson won a Grey Cup with the Stampeders and is a lawyer in Calgary who doubles as an LDS elder.

LESSONS LEARNED ARE HARD TO SHAKE

Keith Holliday, a Dinos linebacker in the 1980s, believes that Coach Connellan's legacy went far beyond wins and losses. The number of Dinos who became coaches shows the effect football had on them. Kadatz and Connellan preached the necessity of giving back to the community, as they must always represent the values they had learned as players. Holliday used the TEAM acronym (together everybody achieves more) to train recruits in the fire department. Holliday believed the "why" behind everyone's actions on the team made them more effective.

Holliday recalled how defensive coordinator Tom Higgins made them learn the responsibilities of everyone on the defence. Players needed to know their jobs, but they also had to know how they fit into the bigger picture. Players were given tests where they were asked to detail their responsibilities in various defences and situations. On their first test, they were graded, and much to their chagrin, they all failed because they didn't detail the responsibilities of everyone on the defence. Higgins, like Connellan, wished to improve the team and in doing so left a legacy of knowledgeable players who would be welcome on any coaching staff.

The head of the Dinos' athletic department in the late 1980s was Bob Corran. He echoed the beliefs of his predecessor, Dennis Kadatz: "It is one of our objectives to develop amateur sports at all levels . . . and the high schools are a big part of that. The attitude they bring to the U of C directly results from some of the people who run high school programs. They get a certain work ethic and an incredible commitment to excellence. With that comes a certain responsibility for us to assist schools whenever they need it."

The Dinos of the 1980s created a legacy that is still felt in Calgary. Everybody in the community is still aware of Connellan. As Holliday recalls, "So many ex-Dinos were coaching. Once, Peter was watching his grandson on his birthday. It was a minor game level, and both teams' coaches had roots with Connellan, so the coaches had the boys run to the stands and sing 'Happy Birthday'!"

Connellan and Kadatz both believed that the university owed it to the community from which they earned a living to give back to it. For Connellan, that meant that the team would almost exclusively be players from Calgary and southern Alberta.

According to Jack Neumann, Connellan had a reputation with coaches in Calgary as a great coach and an even better person. Neumann felt that the Dinos owned the southern half of the province regarding recruiting. Spoletini reflected on his journey to the Dinos: "When I got my phone call from Pete, I felt bad 'cause going to the U of C was kind of like winning a consolation award, but when I met with Pete and the other recruits, I would have turned down the University of Southern California! I was like, wow, I want to stay home."

GO WEST, YOUNG MILES, AND YOU TOO, PETER

It is good for Alberta that Connellan betrayed his ancestral roots in Saskatchewan or we might not have had that fantastic Grey Cup run in the 1950s. As a young teenager, Connellan had a role in getting Rollie Miles to Edmonton. Miles was playing with the Regina Caps, which was a touring baseball team in Western Canada, when he met Connellan for the first time. Peter offered Miles a free newspaper, and a conversation ensued in which Miles promised to watch Connellan and his friends practise. Connellan remembered Miles asking him after several practices if Regina had a professional football team. Connellan took Miles to the Riders' practice field. When Coach Harry Smith came over, Miles asked him for a tryout. Smith replied that the roster was full. Connellan liked Miles and wished he had been given a chance to play for the Riders. The young newspaper boy was sensitive to the fact that, if allowed to play, Miles would have been the only Black player on the team.

Harry Smith's mistake in dismissing Miles was a golden opportunity for the recently formed Eskimos. The day after meeting Smith, Connellan last saw Miles as the Regina Caps went on a road trip to Edmonton. While in Edmonton, a reporter named Don Fleming alerted the Eskimos that Rollie Miles was a young player in town. Annis Stukus could tell an athlete when he saw one and signed him on the spot. Regina cannot say that the fifteen-year-old Connellan did not try.

Like Miles, Connellan headed northwest but for different reasons. Connellan's junior career was short with the Regina Rams as he entered the University of Alberta in the Faculty of Physical Education in the fall after graduating from high school. Peter was in the first-ever graduating physical education class and benefited greatly from Dr. Maury Van Vliet and the faculty he had assembled. As a student at the U of A, Connellan coached junior boys basketball at Scona while playing hockey for the Bears under Hockey Hall of Fame coach Clare Drake.

CALGARY'S GOOD FORTUNE

The Faculty of Physical Education at the University of Alberta was in its formative stages and quickly assembled an elite group of instructors. Dr. Van Vliet was a tremendous leader and an unapologetic advocate for having strong athletic programs in high schools and on campus. According to Van Vliet, coaches had a unique opportunity to instill the virtues of hard work, punctuality, leadership, and teamwork. Connellan felt that Van Vliet viewed those values as crucial in the foundation of the team and the larger society. The work for graduates did not end when they walked the stage to receive their degrees but continued into whatever future they embraced.

A value-based education based on high standards has worked in different parts of Alberta at different times. The successes of the early graduates from the first faculty of physical education inspired others to create winning programs in Alberta and across Canada. Van Vliet expected graduates to model courage and sensitivity. These attributes can only come with a certain degree of confidence in oneself and the knowledge of success. After graduation, Dennis Kadatz and Peter Connellan headed south on Highway 2 to the provincial rival.

A significant loss for the future of Edmonton football was to let Kadatz and Connellan leave. Soon after graduation, Connellan was offered a job in Innisfail to initiate a football program, and he jumped at the chance. In his second year, Innisfail won the central Alberta championship. Kadatz and Connellan soon linked up in Calgary, and the duo began their lifelong journey as friends and colleagues.

Very quickly, they saw the inauguration of the University of Calgary from the former University of Alberta at Calgary, the first Dinos football team, and the establishment of a brilliant athletic department under the leadership of Dr. Goodwin. In 1975 the two coached together at the U of C, and in 1983, Kadatz told Connellan to get his application in for the vacant football coach position for which he was hired shortly after. The duo had little sympathy for their alma mater, and Dinos football ruled the Alberta football scene for nearly four decades. Kadatz and Connellan were friends and a formidable team, and the community reaped the benefits.

An important aspect of the Dinos' success in the 1980s and 1990s was the team's relationship with the Stampeders. An example of this was future CFL Coach of the Year Tom Higgins, who, after retiring as a player from the CFL, volunteered with the Dinos in 1982. Three years later, he signed on with the Stampeders as an assistant and coached the defensive line. The defensive line included former Dinos Stu Laird and Kent Warnock.

The members of Calgary's football community relied on one another for support and professional development. McMaster graduate and eventual head coach Tony Fasano of the Dinos always felt welcome at the Stamps' clubhouse. The Stampeder coaches were always available when Tony faced problems regarding teaching fundamentals or scheming against a particular opponent. Wally Buono, a five-time Grey Cup Champion who retired with 254 coaching wins (a league record), was especially good at answering the questions from the Dinos coaches. The long-term stability of the Stamps and

Dinos' coaching staff provided the Calgary football community with a treasure trove of expertise.

The Alberta football community was always at the forefront of the Dinos' strategic planning. Coach Fasano initiated a coaches' conference that became the biggest in Canada. Fasano recalled, "We put a two-day program together and had a beer and pizza night. They might get thirty or forty out in Ontario, but we got over three hundred some years!" The conferences included coaches from the CFL, high school, university sports, and the NCAA ranks. Frank Solich from Nebraska and Jeff Tedford from the University of California were notable presenters who made big impressions on their audiences.

As the role of the Dinos in Alberta's football community grew, so did the team's financial needs. Kadatz knew that a change in government could leave athletics with a funding problem. Rather than leave the Dinos' finances to the whims of elected officials, Connellan and Kadatz organized an inaugural fundraising dinner with a few parents at the Danish Canadian Club. Jack Neumann recalls it started small, maybe making a couple of thousand dollars, but in time "The Fifth Quarter" has become one of Canada's best football alumni dinners.

At the first dinner, the Dinos were lucky enough to host George Reed and reporter Jim Coleman as the speakers. In 2022 Jack stated, "This year we had Rocky Bleier, former Pittsburgh Steeler, Vietnam War Veteran, and Super Bowl winner speak, and we made two hundred thousand dollars with matching grants." The Dinos' endowment sits at over three million dollars, and community support shows no sign of slowing.

A former Dino pointed to the following stats as evidence of Calgary football culture: since 1948 and the founding of the Stampeders, there has been at least one Calgary high school product on the Stamps. In seventy-five years of pro sports in Calgary, there have been eighty-three Calgarians on the Stamps. There are also dozens of Dinos on team rosters around the CFL, which is a credit not only to the Dinos but also to the high school teams and Calgary minor football. Dr. Van Vliet's community-based vision lives on in Calgary.

DINOS ROOTS IN HUSKIES' HOUSE

The 1950s Edmonton Huskies provided the model for the 1960s Huskies and 1980s Dinos. In 1954 the Huskies Athletic Association was formed, partly in response to the beatings that the Maple Leaf Wildcats gave the South Side Athletic Club and their Southside Oilers for the previous three years. In rebranding the Southside Oilers, Charles Henderson renamed them the Huskies. Henderson, Don McColl, and Tom Shymka were instrumental in getting 250 paid members and 25 men on the board of directors.

The goal of the newly founded Huskies was not just to beat their crosstown rivals but also to become a pillar of the community. Henderson did not mince words when he said, "A boy who plays for the Edmonton Huskies will not only be well equipped and coached but also taught how to be a Canadian citizen." Henderson's language describing the outcome that he and the board would be working toward was direct and in keeping with the consensus in post-WWII Canada. Only nine years after WWII ended, communities in Canada looked forward to a peaceful, productive future.

The Edmonton Huskies Athletic Association's contributions soon formed basketball and track and field teams. In the 1960s and 1970s, the association played a lead role in securing funds for junior and bantam football. In the fall, the Huskies volunteered their time to a one-day blitz where each player filled his car with bantam players and chocolates to be sold door to door.

THE UNUSUAL EDUCATION OF A BUSINESSMAN

The crosstown team that prompted the end of the Southside Oilers' existence was the Edmonton Maple Leaf Athletic Club. One member of the Maple Leafs in the early 1950s was Jack Rutherford, who became a successful businessman, civic leader, and general manager of the Edmonton Wildcats. Jack witnessed the rise of junior football in the 1950s and 1960s. Rutherford viewed his involvement with the Edmonton Maple Leaf Athletic Club as a kind of post-secondary education. Later renamed the Edmonton Wildcats, the

107

Maple Leafs were the team to beat in Edmonton for many years in the early 1950s.

The first-generation Canadian players who made up the Cats were from generally less affluent backgrounds than their opposition south of the river. The rivalry was intense, and each won their share of national championships.

Having decided at the age of fifteen that there was little that Victoria Composite High School had to offer a worldly teenager like himself, Rutherford dropped out and took the initial steps toward a rewarding business career. Eventually, Rutherford found himself as the Western Canada sales manager of Molson. If ever there was a formula for becoming famous, Rutherford saw it in his new role. A friendly young man with unlimited access to one of the finest beers in the world wasted no time getting acquainted with the influencers of the day across Alberta.

Rutherford had no trouble getting invited to all sorts of events, and along the way he met the men he had competed against and some of the finest coaches ever to wear a whistle. The tuition fee that Rutherford paid to attend the school of sport was simply the refreshments he provided to his teachers. His teachers were the émigré from the University of Alberta who were now getting Dinos Athletics whipped into shape. In many ways, Rutherford's handling of employees and the promotion of his product paralleled the principles that Dennis Kadatz, George Kingston, Clare Drake, and Peter Connellan used with their faculties, schools, and teams. Rutherford recalled how he used to socialize with those men for hours and discuss topics relating to team and competition. The discussions were fascinating for Rutherford, as his challenges in business were similar to those of Alberta's greatest coaches. It is safe to say that Jack also had something to offer the coaches in those discussions, and a natural dynamic developed between the young businessman and Alberta's coaching elite.

Leadership demands a vision that sometimes gets lost with people close to the action, such as coaches. Sometimes it takes an administrator or management to shake an organization up. Some examples of this include the Comets' move to twelve-man football or board members hiring a twenty-two-year-old (Kadatz) to coach the Huskies. The Comets' move to twelve-man football was seen as foolhardy by many, as was hiring a twenty-two-year-old to coach twenty-year-olds. Rutherford believed that coaches and people in general need help in seeing the bigger picture in sports and in life. Rutherford's mantra was always that bigger is better—size matters.

An example of daring to dream big occurred in 1959/1960 when the Huskies and Wildcats played out their crosstown rivalry on Wednesday nights. Wildcat manager Jack Rutherford and the president of the Huskies, Don Hamilton, vowed to get 10,000 fans into Clarke Stadium. Both men knew they needed a gimmick, so Rutherford went to Zane Feldman, a local business leader, and asked for a free car to raffle off. Feldman flinched, so Rutherford made the compromise "that it didn't have to be new as long as it ran." Hamilton got a body shop guy to spruce it up, and they drove it up and down Jasper Avenue broadcasting the big game with a chance to win a car. Rutherford recalled, "In those days, you could phone around and get some support. We didn't get ten grand, but we got nine thousand people to attend! You have to think big—always."

MBAS COME IN MANY FORMS

Another businessman from a different century, Chris Lewis, a former Dino, amplified Rutherford's sentiments when he said, "Our province was built on innovation and creativity. Let's take responsibility for the future instead of waiting for the next big thing. Our city didn't have the guts to go for the 2026 Olympics. The last one put us in great shape for thirty years with the volunteerism, spirit, facilities, and legacies." The "last one" Lewis spoke of was the 1988 Winter Olympics, the most successful games in the history of the Olympic movement.

In the early 1980s, Calgary was hardly the international business centre it is today, but many former Eskimos, Huskies, and Dinos were at the forefront of the 1988 Olympics bid. Men like former

Eskimos Peter Lougheed and Don Getty were the most visible, but people like Kadatz worked behind the scenes to ensure the details were taken care of. The status the event brought to Calgary was hard to measure, but the legacy of Olympic facilities that volunteerism made possible lasted a generation.

The success of the Calgary games was not surprising to Rutherford as he had spent hours with the organizers several years before, absorbed their philosophy, and witnessed their accomplishments. Rutherford's hiring bias was finding former athletes who could work with and knew the value of embracing a team philosophy. In practical terms, the dress code of the Huskies or Dinos manager Mike Newans reflected pride that rubbed off on everyone. Kadatz and the Huskies directors demanded that the team wear suits and jackets on road trips. The dress code had practical applications. Perception matters, and personal grooming goes a long way in creating an impression. The old "dress good, feel good" adage makes sense, as leaders must tend to their message and their appearance.

Hall of Fame cornerback Deion Sanders echoed the beliefs that those early Huskies coaches preached when he said, "If you look good, you feel good, and if you feel good, you play good." One should pay attention to successful people's habits as they become the behaviours they use to achieve success. The psychology behind the belief that presenting yourself in a complimentary manner matters is not new and deserves more attention.

In his book *12 Rules for Life*, Dr. Jordan Peterson discusses the physical and psychological necessity of standing tall with your shoulders back and gazing straight ahead. The slouching person with poor posture who avoids eye contact sends a message that life may overwhelm them—hardly the kind of person you would choose to be on your team. When you stand tall, Peterson says, "You respond to challenges instead of bracing for a catastrophe. You see the gold the dragon hoards instead of shrinking in terror from the all-too-real fact of the dragon."

When Deion Sanders showed up to work, there was no doubt in anybody's mind that he meant business that day. For men like him,

Jack Rutherford, and Dr. Murray Smith, along with his many proteges, the business of life begins when you pull your socks on in the morning after making your bed. As Mark Twain said, "You only get one chance to make a first impression."

THE HUSKIES' EMPHASIS ON COMMUNITY MATTERS

One of Rutherford's star employees was a former Huskie named Marv Roberts, a star player recruited by Don McColl and Norm Kimball out of central Alberta. The Derrick Golf and Country Club hosted the recruits. Speaking at the banquet was Murray Smith, who coached the Huskies before handing the reins over to Norm Kimball. Dr. Smith's words profoundly affected Marv, and he developed a lifelong appreciation for Smith's philosophy of sport. Over time Marv found that the Huskies embraced Smith's ethos, which proved to be a formula for success. Service to the community was an essential piece of Huskies pride.

Finding accommodation was an obvious concern for out-of-town Huskies. Roberts fondly remembers his landlady, Mrs. Calloway, who ran a boarding house on 93rd Street and 103rd Avenue. The inconvenience of having four young men late for dinner every night because of practice was something she could put up with under one condition: that they would come with her and her children once a week to play cribbage at the CNIB (Canadian National Institute for the Blind).

Roberts obliged his landlady but did not know what to expect, as playing cards with blind people seemed complicated. Little did he realize it at the time, but Mrs. Calloway kickstarted a lifelong commitment to community service. Roberts grew to love the CNIB and said, "Once you have been down there, you were hooked. I do a lot of volunteer work to this day and I probably wouldn't be doing it if it wasn't for Mrs. Calloway." The CNIB was on Jasper Avenue, and there were ten to twelve blind players and an equal number of sighted players. Most of the blind players were very good and earned Roberts' respect. His work with the CNIB genuinely touched him, and he eventually learned braille.

When the Saskatchewan Roughriders were in danger of folding several years back, Roberts, then a regional manager for Molson in Regina, and several local business leaders in Regina came to the rescue with money and countless hours of volunteerism. An interesting side effect of volunteerism is that the volunteer sometimes benefits more than the recipient of the volunteer's services.

Every community needs more people like Roberts and the Huskies board of directors (current or past). Current board member Mike Eurchuk, whose roots go back to the early 1960s, states that the board of the late 1950s and early 1960s was the finest in Huskies history. Eurchuk viewed the board as men striving to improve their community through volunteerism. Strong, values-based teams create winners both on and off the field. The Huskies' success was duly noted and was a source of civic pride.

Wally Cross, a reporter from the *Edmonton Journal*, created the following jingle after the Huskies won their first national championship 7–3 over Montreal in 1962: "Ring out the bells, sing it loud and lusty, the Leafs are dead. Long live the Huskies."

Denise Kadatz, Dennis's wife, fondly remembers the enormous impact that the first Huskies national title had on the city of Edmonton. She proudly displays in her living room a beautiful silver tray that the City of Edmonton gave to her and Dennis at the reception held after the season. The city's gratitude toward the young couple was still appreciated six decades later.

Hundreds of grateful Edmontonians greeted the Huskies at the train station after their victories over the Rods in the Western Final and the Leafs in the Dominion Final. As Wally Cross reported in November 1962, "Western Champions return home to hundreds of welcomers. The Canadian Junior Football Association pays expenses for a party of 32, including coaches. Still, Huskies are determined they won't go anywhere unless they can take their full team: injured players, mascot, Club President, the works."

The same dilemma faced the Dinos in 1983, and the players found a way to do what the Huskies did twenty-one years earlier. Where the Huskies found support from the business community, each Dino in

1983 donated $50 to ensure their teammates could get to the Vanier Cup in Toronto. The thought of leaving their teammates behind was never an option.

THE TIES THAT BIND

Friendships are an obvious by-product of athletics. As we saw in Calgary, they usually emerge between coaches and administrators, but sometimes coaches make lasting bonds with players. The inordinate amount of time coaches and players spend together creates life-changing conditions for everybody involved. For some, the team and the coach become a surrogate family.

Former QB under Bob Dean, Bo Jereniuk, had a decades-long run as head coach at M.E. LaZerte High School. Jereniuk's players quickly realized that their coach's obsession with athletics was shared by his wife when she set up a highly successful parent association for the football team. Like all the coaches in this book, the Jereniuks were a formidable team. Coach Jereniuk was one of the lucky ones when, in 1980, he met and fell in love with the perfect match in Halyna Hrach. Halyna felt the same way and fell for her "singing Cossack," who was a star on the field and in the Ukrainian men's choir. Later that year, Bohdan and Halyna wed and became a driving force in Edmonton athletics.

Bo never gave up his connection to football, and Halyna prospered in her role as the unofficial M.E. LaZerte general manager and founder of the Voyageur Parent Group. The thousands of dollars that Halyna helped raise gave hundreds of young men the chance to travel across North America. She never resented the late nights of coaching, missed suppers, and difficult nights after losses where sleep was difficult. The Jereniuks went to great lengths to make LaZerte players feel like Paleniuk, Schwartzberg, and Jereniuk did under the mentorship of Bob Dean. Halyna and Bo were a match made in heaven, and northeast Edmonton still reaps the benefits.

At 8:15 p.m. on July 22, 2022, Halyna succumbed to ALS, and Bo found himself alone. The reality of this debilitating disease doesn't fully prepare one for the inevitable outcome. Finding himself alone, Bo put her belongings in a box and worked his way to his vehicle. The shock of what just occurred and the finality of Halyna's passing began to overwhelm Bo, and he recalled that he was hardly in any shape to navigate his way home and face his first night without her. As he entered the hospital parking lot, he heard a voice calling his name and turned to see two of his former athletes, Ed Joseph and Ansar Bacchus. The two men had been on their way to Halyna's room to ensure their coach was okay, as they had heard her prognosis was not good.

Bo, Ed, and Ansar stayed together that night and into the following day. What they spoke about did not matter as much as the fact that they were present. Months later, Bo could not find the words for how much that meant to him and how it validated his and other coaches' daily work. Ed and Ansar offered Bo a slim ray of light on that tragic night and were a tribute to the Jereniuks' sacrifices in building a better community.

The principles and values of loyalty, friendship, and courage that manifested that night are profound and must be nurtured and witnessed by young people. The dedication and kindness shown by Ed and Ansar mirrored the relationship that Bo experienced with his coach and mentor, Bob Dean. Men aspiring to a standard are of immeasurable benefit to a community of young people. The stories of the dozens of men in this book are united through universal truths that football can reveal and facilitate.

THOSE AMAZING ESKS

The Green and Gold of the 1950s occupy a unique position in Alberta's sports history. Professional teams across Western Canada, particularly Edmonton, have all enjoyed success in Grey Cup finals. Still, none have achieved the off-the-field success and community involvement of the 1950s Eskimos. The ongoing goal of any community is to become a better version of themselves. Still, unless organizations and institutions are aware of a community's needs, little of value can be achieved. The Eskimos' long history in Alberta has produced many great teams and citizens but none like those 1950s teams.

The men who played for the Eskimos from 1954–1956 eventually retired and grew into middle age, as did the province. Those Eskimos helped propel Alberta to dizzying heights as a socio-economic power-house. To put the province's growth into perspective, Edmonton's population in 1955 was a paltry 270,000. During the mid-1950s, Edmonton's potential was understood by investors who opened Westmount Mall, one of the first shopping centres in Canada. The arts also benefited from the gains made in the "New West." After Jubilee Auditorium opened in 1957, the Edmonton Symphony Orchestra and the Edmonton Civic Opera found new lodgings. Soon after that the demand for technicians and skilled tradespeople precipitated the Northern Alberta Institute of Technology (NAIT) opening in 1960.

Canada was finding its place on the world stage in the late 1950s as a leader of the middle powers in the postwar world. Canada had tremendous influence in foreign affairs under Prime Minister Lester Pearson, who won the Nobel Peace Prize for his work in the Middle East. Pearson's vision for Canada aligned us closely with the goals of the United Nations and our Western allies, chiefly Great Britain and the United States. America's arrival as a postwar power turned the spotlight onto racial problems that needed to be resolved.

The rise of the American Civil Rights Movement in the 1950s had the unintended consequence of putting Canadian football on the sporting map. Many Black athletes were given opportunities in Canada to make a living that were often unavailable in the United States. Alberta was the beneficiary of many great American football players during the early 1950s.

THE "ESQUIMAX'S" ROOTS

Edmonton's experience with football began early in Alberta's pioneering era when the "Esquimax from the North," as a reporter called them in 1882, played a team from Calgary. To put this into historical perspective, this game predated the Northwest Rebellion of 1885. The population of Edmonton was only 263 people and was vastly outnumbered by its southern rival, Calgary, which boasted a population of 19,500.

In the first decade of the twentieth century, Edmonton was fortunate to have an entrepreneurial American named Deacon White reside in the northern capital. Hailing from Chicago, he formed the Eskimos football team in 1908. White also coached and managed hockey and baseball teams under the Eskimos trademark. Sports played a prominent role in the city's history in the early days of its existence.

White was a real character, which showed when he fought with the Edmonton 49th Battalion in WWI. White was older than the typical recruit, so his fellow 49ers were reluctant to let him see action when deployed to Europe. Growing tired of the preferential treatment, White got an assignment that saw him dodge a few bullets intended for him. As White returned to the trench, the breathless sports team owner remarked that it was more exciting than playing ball!

The period after the Great War saw the province's population grow exponentially. Alberta grew from 73,022 in 1901 to 588,454 in 1921. Edmonton grew to 58,000 citizens, which was eclipsed by Calgary's population of 63,300 in 1921. With a larger population and economy, Alberta football teams now competed for the right to represent Alberta nationally. In 1921 the Eskimos defeated the Calgary Tigers 72–2 and earned the chance to represent the West at Varsity Stadium in Toronto.

The 1921 Edmonton team was the first gridiron group from west of the Great Lakes to challenge for Lord Grey's Cup. Edmonton lost 22–0 to Toronto, but the following year they returned to the Grey Cup with a name change from the Eskimos to the current namesake—the Elks. The Elks Association sponsored the team in 1922, hence the name change.

The travel for the 1922 Cup was unbearable by today's standards and would have the current CFL Players' Association calling their lawyers. It took the Elks four days and four nights to get to Kingston. They arrived at midnight the day of the game. The game was tight at halftime, but Queen's prevailed 13–1. The Elks refused to participate in the social event after the game in protest of the officiating. If the league used eastern officiating crews, one member of the Elks said they would have to be twice as good as their opponents to win.

The players were equally unimpressed with their equipment, and many avoided wearing the dilapidated helmets. Future NHL commissioner Clarence Campbell, a graduate of Strathcona High School, was a player on the 1922 Elks and later put his professional experience to good use. Campbell graduated from the University of Alberta and Oxford University and retired as commissioner of the NHL in 1975 after serving for nearly two decades.

The Eskimos had an on-again, off-again existence until 1949. The success of the Stampeders in the 1948 Grey Cup was too much for business leaders in Edmonton. Walter Sprague was instrumental in bringing community leaders together and reviving the team. Hall of Fame columnist Terry Jones quoted Walter Sprague as saying in 1948, "Those cow towners won the Cup, and we weren't even in the League!" The population of Edmonton was 137,000 at the time. Dr. Maury Van Vliet of the University of Alberta sold equipment and uniforms to the Eskimos for $4,000. To put that into perspective, at the time, Coca-Cola was a nickel. The green and gold of the U of A became the green and gold of the Eskimos.

The choice of "Eskimos" as the team name was controversial in 1949. One Edmonton columnist said the name was ridiculous, as no Inuit or Eskimo settlement was within 1,000 miles of Edmonton. The directors considered the name "Oilers," but "Eskimos" prevailed. The team colours were appropriate owing to the poplar and ever-green fall colors. Whatever the motives for returning professional football to Edmonton, the Eskimos were a positive force in the city and the province.

Ideally, professional sports teams impact communities beyond merely entertaining them. High-profile athletes' potential for drawing attention to critical areas of concern are well known. Sometimes athletes can become chairpersons of charities. Other times their donations of time and money can make a massive difference to important causes. A friendly nod or an encouraging word from a sports star can make a big difference for a suffering child or adult. There is, however, the issue of mistakes that athletes sometimes make off the field.

COMMUNITY'S THE THING

Former Eskimo and Hall of Famer Tom Wilkinson firmly believed that professional athletes were responsible to the community as individuals of character who would inspire others. Wilkinson said all adults are responsible for giving young people a positive role model or mentor. Men like Wilkinson, Pop Ivy, and Annis Stukus were keenly aware that the actions of sports stars impact communities.

High school, junior, and university programs can only speculate on the effectiveness of their programs in producing adults with character, as the fruits of their labour only become apparent after a few years. Former UCLA basketball coach John Wooden often said the team's goal was to win a championship, but he would not know for several years after the players graduated what kind of job he had done as a coach and mentor. Kareem Abdul-Jabbar said it best: "Coach John Wooden taught me that sports weren't just about making us better athletes, but about making us better people."

The Eskimos players often had families and careers underway and were on a trajectory that would propel many to leadership roles in their community. The extent of the impact of the 1950s Grey Cup teams deserves attention, as the Edmonton teams later provided the leadership Coach Wooden would have hoped for from graduates of his program. Wooden's goal of building better men did not detract from his goal of winning championships, as he won ten national crowns at UCLA.

The roots of Edmonton's 1950s team were laid in 1949 by a flamboyant native of Ontario whose foresight set the stage for decades of football greatness in Alberta. That first coach of the 1949 team was Annis Stukus, and he proved to be more than "just" a legendary promoter from Toronto. When Stukus signed his players to contracts, he appointed them to coach at specific high schools. Players were expected to give back to the community, so they volunteered their time with amateur football.

High school programs got a boost from having the pros put them through their paces, as did the Eskimos' box office, with a legion of new fans clamouring to see their stars who doubled as coaches. The genius of Stukus was in recognizing that the professional league's future fans would come from the relationships formed on the field after school between men from all over North America and the youth of Edmonton.

Canadians were the strength of that 1949 team, including future Premier Peter Lougheed, Member of Parliament Steve Paproski, and international wrestling star Gene Kiniski. The club's directors deemed the American recruits to be of terrible quality. One American named Radovich weighed 450 pounds, which was unheard of in a league where 180-pound linemen were commonplace. The situation regarding talent from south of the border would soon change as the Eskimos tapped into the Oklahoma Sooner pipeline by hiring young coaches Darrell Royal in 1953 and Pop Ivy in 1954.

ALBERTA WAS A DESIRED DESTINATION

Royal and Ivy came from Sooner royalty, and their winning ways followed them north. They were clear on what the conduct of professional athletes should look like on the field and in the locker room. The formula for the Eskimos was much like the one employed by Wooden at UCLA, and the results were similar.

After 1949, the Eskimos became ingrained in the Edmonton community. John Belmont, a Football Alberta Hall of Fame member, migrated west from Quebec with his parents in the early 1950s. He remembered the Green and Gold as a source of nightly entertainment. John's mother would pack supper, and the family would jump in the car and head to practice to watch some of the best players in North America. Economic and social reasons enticed Americans like Bright, Miles, Anderson, Parker, Dean, and Walker.

The fact that so many Americans stayed in the off-season added to the fanaticism of Edmontonians for their team. Social and business relationships between the players and fans were everywhere in the provincial capital.

Adding to the excitement were Albertans playing alongside collegiate players from the US. The Albertans on the 1956 Grey Cup team were impressive: Mike Kmech, Oscar Kruger, Don Simon, Bill Smith, Normie Kwong, Don Barry, Laurie Hodgson, Steve Bendiak, Con Kelly, Leigh McMillan, Mike King, Jim Shipka, and Steve Mendryk. The locals were a source of great pride for local fans and players.

Many of the Canadians who came west liked what they experienced and stayed. Getty's arrival from the University of Western Ontario pushed Jackie Parker from QB into the backfield, where Ivy hoped he could add an explosive element to an already great offence. The Eskimos looked unstoppable with Bright and Kwong as twin fullbacks and Miles and Parker as wingbacks. The move by Pop Ivy was somewhat controversial, and the team's prankster, Normie Kwong, made the most of it. Edmonton reporter Terry Jones reported that a week before the 1956 Grey Cup, Normie Kwong jokingly told Don Getty that if they did not win the Cup, Kwong would have Getty's opium supply cut off. Luckily for the Eskimos and Getty's future political aspirations, the Green and Gold won Lord Grey's Cup and Getty began his career on a good note.

A graduate of Western Ontario with deep roots in Quebec and Ontario, Getty became a transplanted Westerner in 1955. Getty never regretted jumping in an old blue Buick with high school sweetheart Margaret Mitchell and heading west. Alberta was lucky to get the pair, who were instrumental in changing Alberta's political landscape. Getty and Lougheed formed a formidable political team in their post-football careers. They managed to lead the Conservative Party to a victory in 1971 over the Social Credit Party, which had been in power since 1935.

Well-educated, community-minded, and ambitious, the young Conservative Party had deep roots in Alberta and its sporting community. The Conservatives proved especially important in the 1980s when Calgary needed support to help its ailing Stampeders and to win the right to host the 1988 Winter Olympics.

With a population under 200,000 in the early 1950s, one can imagine attracting players who wanted to be big fish in a small pond, but those Americans who came north were big fish from huge ponds. Frank Anderson was an all-American from Oklahoma who was enticed north by then-manager Al Anderson. On the field, "old blood and guts" was a perennial all-star, but once his career ended, he became even more valuable for his contributions off the field as a businessman and philanthropist. His insurance business was very successful and allowed him to donate time and money to the board of Winnifred Stewart and the United Way. He also served as chair of the Salvation Army.

Arguably one of the best athletes ever to represent Edmonton on and off the field was a native of Toronto, Frank Morris, who, like Getty, came west and never returned. After serving a brief stint in the Canadian Navy, his sense of "team" was forged with the Argos, whom he described as a group that partied hard and played hard. Morris, one of the Eskimos' captains, applied the same formula in Edmonton. The results followed. Frankie was a much-loved figure in the Edmonton sporting community for over fifty years. Frank was also an ardent supporter of the arts community in Edmonton and was seen frequently at operas and symphonies.

The coach of the 1953 Edmonton team was Darrell Royal, who enjoyed nineteen stellar years with the Texas Longhorns. Edmonton benefited immensely from the Miles family's decision to stay in Alberta after his retirement. Some say Miles's substantial contributions to the sporting community were surpassed by his impact on education in Edmonton's Catholic School District as a teacher and later as a supervisor. Rollie's wife, Dr. Marianne Miles, had an equally distinguished career as an educator, administrator, and professional psychologist.

THE ESKIMOS' GIFT TO ALBERTA

The backfield of Kwong and Bright had an enduring effect on the province long after their playing days were finished. Kwong returned to Calgary after his playing career ended. His imprint on Calgary grew to include being the president of the Stampeders and bringing the Flames from Atlanta to Calgary. Kwong is one of the few men with his name on the Stanley Cup and the Grey Cup. His service to the province of Alberta as the lieutenant governor was the ultimate testimony to Albertans' affection and respect for the man born in Calgary.

Johnny Bright spent his playing days practising in the evenings, playing on the weekends, and delighting his students during the day. Like Miles and Dean, Bright was a professional educator who excelled as an administrator. He was drafted in the first round by the Philadelphia Eagles, ran track, and played fastball and basketball. The Harlem Globetrotters offered him a contract, as did the Philadelphia Eagles, but the Stampeders' offer was higher. Blair Bennett remembers the star power Bright carried as "he swaggered down the hallways of Bonnie Doon. He was larger than life. Before the games he'd look at each player with big eyes and ask, 'Are you ready?' A reply was necessary before he would go on to the next guy!"

Another American who came north and substantially impacted Edmonton was Bob Dean. Beyond his football prowess, Dean was an excellent principal with Edmonton Public Schools who also found the time to be a school trustee, leader of the Shriners, and member of the police commission. Dean's embrace of his new community was complete and absolute, and Edmonton was fortunate to have him.

Bob was also a distinguished violinist and was offered a music scholarship to Carnegie Mellon in Pittsburgh. He remained a lifelong supporter of the arts and always encouraged his players to participate in school arts programs. The Opera Society of Edmonton could always count on the Dean family's support.

Stukus must have been very proud of the legacy his foresight in 1949 helped produce. One *Edmonton Journal* headline proclaimed the first Grey Cup team members in 1954 "Heroes All—Every Last

One of Them." Former Wildcat and Golden Bear Oscar Krueger became a prominent defence attorney. Al Bryant and Jack Lamb became business leaders, as Steve Mendryk did in academia. Earl Lindley went home to achieve great things as a coach at BYU in Utah.

A BLUEPRINT FOR SUCCESS

The values that guided Alberta's exemplary teams are readily available for any young coach looking for guidance. The Dinos' motto of TEAM (together everyone achieves more) was only as good as it was implemented. The Comets and the Browns had an advantage over other teams as the groups' guiding philosophy had its roots in the spiritual values of the community in which they operated.

Competitive sports have shown us over and over that teams that live and breathe a unifying principle have a better chance at success. The one value that the Comets, Dinos, Huskies, Eskies, and Browns shared was that they owed their accomplishments to putting the team before themselves. The second goal for every program was for the players to use their knowledge to benefit the community.

An essential aspect of community building is the leaders' role in being authentic in their messaging and pursuit of excellence. People are quick to recognize phony or insincere leaders and that, more than anything, can be the death knell of creating cohesive groups. One of the great fears in the programs that still endure as good teams (Comets, Browns, and Dinos) is that they will forget or disregard the reasons for their success. Jack Neumann's belief that houses take a long time to build but can be destroyed quickly is seen repeatedly in sports.

It is only natural that people who have experienced success on a team built on a foundation of community would wish to repeat the same experience for the rest of their lives. Whether in fire halls, businesses, schools, government, volunteerism, or families, the men on these pages have used the lessons learned on the field and in the locker rooms to the community's advantage. Along the way, they inspired many people through their actions to achieve more in their personal and professional lives.

-6-

CHASING PERFECTION

"The greater danger for most of us lies not in setting our aim too high and falling short; but in setting our aim too low, and achieving our mark." – Michelangelo

After our initial meeting in the Raymond High School staff room, I thanked and shook the hands of the five attending gentlemen. As I got up to put my various devices away, Jim Ralph shook my hand and looked me in the eye. "And don't put us at the back of the book!" he said. The rest of the guys laughed, but Jim didn't.

Jim Ralph probably never met Vince Lombardi or anybody who even knew the Packers coach, but he sure nailed one of Lombardi's central tenets when the Raymond coach said, "If you are going to do something in life, be the best you can be. That's not just in athletics; that's in life. It's a competitive world, and you are going into it whether you like it or not." Raymond loves to win, but more importantly, the effort and will to win must be present whenever a Comets jersey gets pulled over one's head. Lombardi, like Ralph, conveyed a similar view on life when he said, "The quality of a man's life is in direct proportion to his commitment to excellence, regardless of his chosen field of endeavour."

One commonality between the five programs was uncovered early in the interviews. The men hated losing more than they liked winning. Losses tore at the men who led these teams. They took it personally.

Teams must work hard to outcoach the Comets, Huskies, Dinos, Browns, and Eskimos.

Raymond's Bob Gibb recalls the effect losing had on him, and it reminds one of something that Washington head coach George Allen once said: "Losing the Super Bowl is worse than death. With death you don't have to get up in the morning." Gibb's winning record as a head basketball and assistant football coach was staggering. At one point, his Comets basketball teams in the mid-1960s won over sixty games in a row. Gibb remembers his wife knowing what to expect after a loss. It meant she would go to bed alone as he would watch TV till the wee hours of the morning. The Gibb family goes back a long way in Raymond and summed up the community's attitude with, "We can't accept anything less than the best."

The founding father of Comets football, Brian Dudley, is a relative newcomer to Raymond, having been there for only five or six decades. Dudley embraced the kind of competitiveness that Raymond covets. "We hated to lose more than we liked to win. We should have won the games we lost. I made mistakes. One game in particular was shattering when we lost to Cardston. I still remember the guys who dropped the balls." Jim Ralph commented on Dudley's recollection of the Cardston game and the effect that losing had on him, saying, "Those are the kind of people we are. We appreciate those kinds of people."

Bob Gibb remembers a basketball game against Bright's Bonnie Doon Lancers in the 1960s when the Comets and the Lancers were the two superpowers of Alberta basketball. The game was played at Lethbridge Collegiate Institute and was very close, with many lead changes. The Comets were stacked with players like the Tollestrup brothers and Lloyd Fairbanks. Eventually, the Comets went up by eight late in the game. Gibb laughed as he recalled Bright's anger as he turned his chair around and refused to watch the game for the last minute when it was clear Raymond would win. Although Gibb saw Bright's actions as humorous, he understood the intensity of Bright's feelings.

Bernie Orr was a longtime Raymond coach who greatly admired Dudley and Raymond's approach to life and athletics. Like Kadatz's teams, the Comets placed a strong emphasis on conditioning. Orr said he didn't want to waver in the fourth quarter. "You do not want to send a kid out to war with a popgun!" Not only did Bernie remember Dudley's emphasis on conditioning, he also remembered him as a great motivator. His pregame speeches would make the hair on the back of Orr's neck stand up.

Ralph played for Dudley as a young man and felt that commitment to practice and fitness were crucial pillars in Dudley's coaching. Attendance at practice was mandatory unless there was a death in the family or something equally serious. Dudley taught Ralph that it was like a heavyweight fight: you would take punches and give some. For Ralph, "It was important to not have a chink in your armour. I felt nobody would knock me down and I would stay down on the teams I played for. Nobody's going to outrun me. Nobody's going to out-stamina me."

Ralph pointed out that after Dudley left the junior high program, the winning did not continue. For Ralph, leadership is essential. Ralph talked about how coaches are critical to a team's success. Great coaches have a crucial role in teaching other coaches. The coach's tree from Bernie Orr and Brian Dudley matters: "Finish first because no one remembers second."

Dudley's assessment of his athletes was surprising. "We were not super-duper athletes, but we got 110 percent out of them." His record of 178 wins, 31 losses, and 2 ties gave him a winning percentage of 83 percent. Rather than dwelling on the successes, Dudley vividly remembers the losses, saying, "I made mistakes!" One hundred and seventy-eight victories weren't enough for Dudley.

The Comets' success at the eight-man level led to a controversial move up to provincial twelve-man football. Dudley states, "Many opposed the idea as they thought we were absolutely going to get killed." As time passed, the Comets enjoyed some local success until they reached a plateau in provincial playoff games against LCI and St. Francis. The much larger schools used playbooks that highlighted their much larger athletes, and Raymond was forced to go back to the drawing board and design a style of play that would draw upon their strengths—quickness, fitness, and athleticism.

"However beautiful the strategy, you should occasionally look at the results." – Winston Churchill

Churchill's famous quotation alludes to generals who refuse to adapt their "brilliant" strategies to changing circumstances or conditions. Still, coaches suffer from a similar malady when they believe their carefully designed playbooks are foolproof and refuse to change.

Of all sports, football is the best suited for coaches to have an immediate impact on the events unfolding in front of them. Every thirty seconds, the coaches call the play, determine what the twelve men on the field will be responsible for, and execute the plan. The following paragraphs critically examine the importance of playbooks and the nuances around executing those plays. Most fans and coaches feel that the X's and O's are relatively simple: you have an inside run, an outside run, a short pass, a deep pass, and a couple of trick plays, and you have an offence.

People are mistaken when they compare football to a game of chess. Artificial intelligence will no doubt be used to design the perfect playbook, but inputting variables will be ever-changing and difficult to stay on top of. Computers can beat chess experts, but football is much more complex as the pieces (players) have human strengths and frailties.

Educated fans often see the mistakes coaches who refuse to change their strategies during a game make. Coaching football is awkward as they demand obedience to a strategy, but plans sometimes must be abandoned after the first punch is thrown. For example, if a running back is dominant, the defence might put their linebackers and defensive backs closer to the line of scrimmage to stop him. In doing so, the defence is vulnerable to the pass. If coaches are slow to recognize a change in tactics by their opposition, they are doomed.

Another all-too-common mistake is that coaches see a championship team like the New England Patriots and copy their offence. The problem is, there is only one Tom Brady. When Raymond returned to the drawing board and did an honest assessment of their team's characteristics, they followed the example set many years before by Coach Dudley when he utilized a finesse-based system in eight-man football.

Some apply the Pareto Principle (twenty percent of people produce eighty percent of the results) to other forms of human endeavours, including sports. When one considers the success of the Dinos, Comets, Browns, Huskies, and Eskimos, one must wonder if the same principle applies to football. All of these teams mastered their playbooks and understood how those plays were run. They did not just copy the ideas of other coaches.

The execution of a playbook depends on players and coaches understanding the "why" behind the play being run. If a coach doesn't understand the details of the playbook, how can the players? One 1960s high school in Edmonton with a long and storied tradition in football had a new coach who used the plays from an American coaching magazine titled "The Best 100 Plays for High School Football." He had a short run as head coach. Winning is hard work, and there are seldom any shortcuts for coaches or players.

BACK TO THE FUTURE

Coaches should look through online videos to give them a historical appreciation for the many offences that have won championships. The present read option, with the QB several yards behind the centre, is a variation of the one-hundred-year-old single wing offence. The single wing allowed for a direct snap to the most gifted athlete on the offence who could run, pass, or hand off the ball.

Single wing principles are used today with teams with skill sets like the legendary Jackie Parker. Today's shotgun offence is a partial throwback to the single wing. Quarterbacks like Tom Brady and Peyton Manning used the shotgun to give them a better view of the defence, not for them to run the ball.

The single wing gave way to split-T and wing-T offences of the 1950s, where the QB became more of a manager and less of a playmaker as he moved his hands under the centre to take the snap. By taking the ball from under the centre, there were fewer fumbles, and more players could be playmakers. Coaches need to understand that every playbook and system of plays has limitations that eventually lead to new developments and variations.

An excellent example of coaches knowing an offence and adapting it to a different set of circumstances was the 1950s Eskimos. The root of the 1950s Eskimos' success was their attention to detail and connection to the winning football played at Oklahoma under Bud Wilkinson. Wilkinson revolutionized college football with the split-T formation.

The split-T featured a QB with three running backs behind him like a T. Wilkinson's approach to playing the split-T was separating players one to four feet apart. The discipline and execution of those great Sooner teams were more important than the configuration of running backs and the offensive line. The split-T became a cultural phenomenon in the early 1950s in America.

Maclean's magazine was so impressed with the Eskimos success in 1954 and 1955 that on September 1, 1956, they ran a feature story that traced the roots of the split-T offence in Canada. Frank Filchock was the Eskimos coach in 1952, and he consulted Wilkinson in Oklahoma to bring his split-T to Canada. Filchock had success taking the Eskimos to the Western Final, then made the mistake of asking GM Al Anderson for more money and a contract extension. Anderson fired Filchock and flew to Oklahoma to visit Bud Wilkinson.

Teams across the USA were eager to adopt Wilkinson's offence, and many looked to his assistant coaches for the answers to their coaching vacancies. Anderson soon found his man in Darrell Royal. The arrival of a Bud Wilkinson protégé was greeted with much fanfare by Eskimos fans. Royal's knowledge of the split-T and Wilkinson's coaching techniques netted him a hefty contract from Anderson, who outbid Mississippi State for his services.

Royal had a unique vision of the role of line play and how to utilize the distance (splits) between the offensive linemen to create an advantage.

In Royal's version of the split-T, linemen were allowed to split wider from their teammates than Wilkinson permitted in Oklahoma. The distance between the centre and the guards varied, as did the split between the guards and tackles. By changing their splits, the offensive linemen on the other side of the play could draw their defensive opposition farther away from the point of attack.

With more space between the linemen, there was more daylight for the running backs. Offensive linemen and running backs had to understand the concept of adjusting splits if the offence was to be successful. The real advantage in the Eskimos' version of the split-T was that those linemen did not have to open holes, as their splits moved the defensive linemen apart. All the linemen had to do was get their heads to one side of their opponent, as it was unnecessary to push defensive linemen off the line of scrimmage like in the single wing or tight-T offences.

Smart, quick linemen were essential to the success of the split-T. Small, muscular, athletic guards were best as they needed to get off the line fast and pull around the end. Canadians were often used at the guard position, as their contracts were inexpensive, and the money saved could be used for higher-priced Americans at the skill positions. Mike Kmech was the prototypical guard in the Wilkinson offence and was offered a scholarship to Oklahoma the year he made the Eskimos. The scholarship was attractive for the farm boy from Lamont but not as much as playing for his hometown.

Ball deception was essential in Royal's offence, and former Sooner QB Claude Arnold was the perfect wizard to run the offence. Ball handling and faking seem to be a lost art today, but in the 1950s it gave defences fits.

Once the ball is snapped, good offences often trick defences as to their true intentions. Bernie Faloney (CFL Hall of Famer) succeeded Claude Arnold as the starting QB in the 1954 Grey Cup and had experience running the split-T at the University of Maryland. Faloney was adept at tricking defences, as were the Eskimos' running backs. On one play, Tex Coulter of the Alouettes tackled Normie Kwong. As the ref went to blow his whistle, Kwong shrieked, "Don't blow it! I haven't got the ball!" Across the field, Faloney, who had faked the handoff to Kwong, tossed it to Parker, who ran for a significant gain.

DIFFERENT COACH, MORE INNOVATION

Pop Ivy succeeded Royal as coach in 1954 and changed the offence to take advantage of the Eskimos' personnel. Ivy lined up the two fullbacks, Kwong and Bright, directly behind the guards. The move to two running backs instead of three allowed Parker and Miles to be the wingbacks lined up outside the ends. This gave the Eskimos an added threat to the outside. Coach Ivy was an Oklahoma grad and disciple of Wilkinson who believed in running a few plays well. Coach Wilkinson converted many high school programs in Oklahoma to his style of football, as Ivy did in Edmonton.

As Ivy quickly learned, "The difference between winning and losing is how well our Canadian players perform. They are the backbone of any squad in Canadian football." Ivy's observations led to the Eskimos supporting a solid minor football program in Edmonton in the 1950s and 1960s.

Bob Dean adopted Ivy's philosophy regarding practice structure and fundamentals to reiterate Jim Ralph's belief in coaches learning from credible mentors. The typical Eskimos practice was a good mixture of tackling, blocking, agility, conditioning, and play running. Eskimos recalled years later how the offence's simplicity allowed the players to learn little things to make it work. An example of this was the hundreds of practice repetitions reinforcing the running backs' timing of receiving the handoff and making a precise cut based on the guard's block. The QBs could vary their cadences and snap count because the group was disciplined and drilled to perfection. Other teams adopted the double fullback system, but none could repeat the Eskimos' successes.

The triple option of the 1960s, made famous by coaches south of the border but practised in the 1950s by Edmonton's professional team, was a return to the base philosophy of the single wing. The thought of an athlete like Jackie Parker handing off to Kwong or Bright up the middle with the option of Parker running outside with Rollie Miles trailing for a potential pitch was a nightmare for a defence. The Eskimos' offence was designed to match the personnel they possessed.

Many coaches imagine their QB to be like Jackie Parker when he is not. The coach's aim should be to design an offence appropriate for their QB's skill set. Don Getty replaced Parker at QB in 1956 and won the Grey Cup. Still, the offence was structured much differently by utilizing the managerial role of the QB and highlighting the skill sets of the players at their skill positions. The small percentage of coaches who consistently win know the capabilities of their players and the advantages of running the appropriate play systems.

> *"He who defends everything defends nothing."*
> *– Frederick the Great*

The same is true of defensive football, where coaches often fall in love with a style or system of play regardless of the circumstances. The great Prussian general Frederick the Great believed that the folly that often befalls defensive coaches is that they refuse to acknowledge that their system has weaknesses. Every defence has a potential weakness, and the defensive coordinator must account for that.

Like all the great offences of the past, all types of defences have won championships. To blitz or not to blitz is a dilemma that defensive coordinators must answer. Committing extra players to the run takes away from pass coverage. More men defending the pass allows the offence to run the ball easier. A sound defence usually has the ability to be flexible in how it attacks the offence.

Whatever offence or defence a team runs, the plays called should never cause indecision or confusion in the players. Players who are hesitant or indecisive will be beaten. Confident, purposeful athletes executing a clear plan have an advantage and play faster. Creating confident athletes is the goal of every coach, and repetition is an important part of this process.

CONNELLAN'S RELENTLESS COMPETITIVENESS

Coaches like Pop Ivy, Gary DeMan, Peter Connellan, Brian Dudley, and Dennis Kadatz faced difficult times, but the essence of their offences changed little over the years. Connellan in particular was a stickler for executing flawlessly the few plays his playbook contained. Rather than add plays to their playbooks, Connellan and DeMan polished their plays through careful coaching.

Connellan's endless pursuit of improving his team began as a high school coach at Viscount Bennett High School. Connellan won many high school championships running a power-I formation with three backs and a tight end. In 1977 he was seconded to the U of C and ran an offence that flopped the right and left sides of the offensive line. He called it a strong and weak side where the players would play on both sides of the centre depending on the play call. If teams favoured the strong side, plays were run to the weak side. Athletic Director Dennis Kadatz told Connellan that he did not like the offensive scheme but later had to admit it was a good idea after the Dinos won the Canada West title in 1977.

Connellan pointed out that he was an American Football Coaches Association member and received all their books and literature. Peter said, "I would take the good articles out, comment on them and give them to a coach and say this is what I want you to do." The inspiration for having a solid and weak side on the offensive line came from former Eskimos coach Darrell Royal, who became the head coach of the University of Texas. After Coach Lashuk's return to the Dinos in 1978, Connellan resumed his duties at Viscount Bennett, and his legendary tussles with DeMan's Browns were renewed.

Connellan once said that he only had to run three offensive plays to win, but execution had to be of the highest grade. The lead, the fake lead play-action pass, and the counter off the lead were the basis of his offence. His thinking was simple: if you were stopping the lead, the fake lead pass or counter would work.

A play Connellan added later was the inside trap from Hall of Fame Coach Tom Osbourne at the University of Nebraska. The trap involves creating angles for the offensive lineman to attack the defensive lineman. The execution of the play is somewhat complex but is potentially tough to defend. Connellan spent a lot of time with Coach Osbourne learning the trap, which was instrumental in helping him to a 0.836 winning percentage and three national championships. Osbourne, like Connellan, DeMan, Kadatz, and Ivy ran a few plays well.

In *The Art of War*, Sun Tzu says, "The whole secret lies in confusing the enemy so that he cannot fathom our real intent." The first step of everyone on the Dinos' offence was the same, so the defence did not have a clue what the play would be until it was too late. The players' first step had to be of the correct angle and distance to achieve the play's success. Connellan was a stickler for reviewing his players' first steps on film when the ball was snapped.

Dinos fullback Tony Spoletini said the coaches would run the lead when they knew the defence was ready to stop it. This deception gave the defence the false belief that the game was in hand. Spoletini said this allowed the QB to fake the lead, run the counter, screen, and play-action passes. Usually, the counters, fake lead play-action, and screens would be run late in the first half or saved for the second half. Even when teams were waiting for the inevitable counters, screens, or play-action pass, they could not stop it.

The offence Connellan eventually settled on consisted of only four plays. But off each play was a draw, a screen, a reverse, and a pass. The variations of the four plays took it to a total of sixteen. "Execution was everything," Spoletini said. "You could do it without thinking." Execution and repetition were the keys to winning.

Contrary to what defensive coordinators preach to their players, the offence dictates the play. Defences can only guess what is about to unfold. Defences scout for tendencies in space calling or look for pre-snap keys that give them an edge. Down and distance are also important cues for the defence.

Connellan and his coaches demanded that the offensive players have strict pre-snap protocols that had to be adhered to, which prevented the defence from any clues as to which play was going to be run. Linebackers love pre-snap keys as they can begin moving early to the area the offence will attack. RBs often need to look at the point of attack before the snap, but if they stare too long at where they are going, LBs can move to that area. An offensive lineman who leans forward in his stance is signifying that it will be a running play. If an offensive lineman is leaning back and ready to stand up, the play will be a pass. The Dinos' offensive coaches were fanatical about getting rid of pre-snap keys.

As mentioned, linebackers were especially vulnerable to the type of offence the Dinos mastered in the 1980s. Positioned behind the defensive line and in front of the defensive backs, they need help to guess right on the play. One or two missteps create huge gaps on the field for the offence to exploit.

The Dinos' running game was characterized by four elements: a strong commitment by the entire unit to block, a crushing fullback, a fleet tailback, and a poised field general at QB. Two former Dinos described Connellan's passing attack as sophisticated as anything they had experienced in the CFL. A good offence is only one aspect of a winning team, and the Dinos defence was equally stellar.

EXECUTION AND FUNDAMENTALS ARE THE KEYS TO VICTORY

Simplicity and preparation were the keys for defensive coordinator Tony Fasano and his staff. Their defensive scheme featured only a couple of blitzes and coverages. Still, it was a defence that contained offences and demanded they make long, error-free drives by being good tacklers, excellent in pursuit, and able to get off blocks. Dinos defenders rarely put defenders on an "island" without a teammate's support. Fasano's defences offered few surprises for opponents, but they were difficult to crack.

The Fasano defence was reminiscent of the Oklahoma defences of the early 1950s. Coach Bud Wilkinson believed in a similar scheme that featured a "contain" unit composed of corners and safety whose job was to keep the ball in front of them and not give up easy touchdowns. The other eight players on the field were the force unit that played more aggressively and attacked the offence with specific responsibilities. The Sooners and the Dinos' defences rarely gambled and could be characterized as defences that "bend but don't break."

*"Intellectual growth should commence at birth and
only cease at death." – Albert Einstein*

Meeting and interacting with the best in any profession is an excellent opportunity for young people, but working alongside the masters of a craft is the ultimate professional development. The magic touch of Kadatz as a coach continued when he became athletic director, where he facilitated the development of his coaches. Fasano noted Kadatz's support for the coaching staff through professional development as essential to the Dinos' success. The year the University of Washington Huskies won the national title with Don James, the Dinos coaching staff travelled to Washington for spring camp. The Dinos coaches had unlimited access to practices and film sessions. Fasano said, "I was intrigued with what they were doing and what we could bring back to Calgary. The foundation of our defence was from the U of W!" Connellan took the Dinos to several universities south of the border.

Professional development was a crucial piece of the Dinos' coaching success. On one coaching trip to learn from the national champion University of Colorado coaching staff, a young Dinos coach, Chris Lewis, had an experience that any young coach would cherish. Lewis was a storied running back with the Dinos, as was his equivalent in Colorado.

The RB coach with the Buffaloes was Eric Bieniemy, who would later go on to coordinate the offence of the Super Bowl–winning Kansas City Chiefs. Bieniemy was so impressed with the foundation of Lewis's coaching that he remarked that Chris knew more about some of the drills than he did, so "go ahead and run them!" In light of Bieniemy's future successes in the NFL, Lewis had one up on any coach in his future that wanted to impress him with his credentials.

If Peter Connellan were coaching south of the border, he would have had the status of a movie star. His coaching record in twelve years at the university level was eight Canada West championships and four national championships. His overall record as a head coach was 87–38–2. His post-season record was a remarkable 16–6 with a winning percentage of 0.727. Connellan's Dinos never finished below

0.500 during his tenure. His teams made the playoffs when only two teams in the Western Conference qualified for the post-season.

"The secret of change is to focus all of your energy,
not on fighting the old, but on building the new." – Socrates

Connellan's mental approach to competition affirms Viktor Frankl's suggestion that "We have absolutely no control over what happens to us in life, but what we have paramount control over is how we respond to those events." Whether it was a big win, a touchdown scored, or some adversity that befell the Dinos, Connellan's focus was unshakeable.

George Paleniuk recalled a game in Edmonton where he focused on the Dinos' bench, hoping to get some insights into the reasons for their success. Paleniuk observed a focus that rivalled that of the St. Francis Browns. After a touchdown, Connellan scribbled in his notebook that there was no inappropriate celebration by the players. The players competed at a high emotional level but were good at maintaining their composure and focus. According to Paleniuk, the players were not looking at the stands, sitting on their helmets, hanging their heads, taking their time getting in and out of the huddle, or seeking unnecessary attention from the trainers.

Paleniuk was astonished by the Dinos' attention to detail. It was a wet, muddy field that day and players who were not dressed were cleaning the mud out of cleats with popsicle sticks, as were the trainers. Water bottles were never half empty, as they were constantly refilled. Non-starters were focused on the field and were always ready for their number to be called. Connellan's focus during the game significantly impacted Paleniuk, as it was a stark contrast to their opponents.

Fans who enjoy the antics of emotional coaches during a game would have been disappointed watching Connellan and his staff. Seeing coaches and/or players throwing things around the sidelines in fits of rage or celebration may be entertaining, but it is also counterproductive. Winning coaches of today, such as Nick Saban (Alabama), Mike O'Shea (Winnipeg), and Bill Belichick (New

England), have very little time for distractions on or off the field. Like Connellan, they focus on preparing for games and executing their game plans. Distractions take away from preparation and working toward winning a championship.

"It is no use saying, 'We are doing our best.' You have got to succeed in doing what is necessary." – Winston Churchill

His voice rising, Mike Newans, Dinos equipment manager, described the team's goal: "We all knew why we were there. The goal was to win, win, win! If you didn't share that goal, get the hell out of here!" When asked if he held a special hatred for his intra-provincial rivals in Edmonton, he paused. "Hate is a strong word, but yes, I hated the Bears. But I hated them all—Thunderbirds, Huskies, and Bisons!" His voice climbing to new heights, he continued, "I felt the same way about Guelph, Western, and Queens. We all hated them." Remember, he was the equipment manager.

Newans contributed to the competitive atmosphere by rewarding the veteran Dinos with the newest equipment. Highly recruited rookies were told to live with the old Riddell helmets, as the veterans got the better Bike ones. Rookies soon learned that they had to compete to earn respect, and nothing was given until that happened. There was a pecking order, and Newans took great pride in motivating the players to be their best.

St. Francis and Utah State graduate Tom Forzani is clear on why he continues to coach after over two decades at Cochrane High School: "A lot of people say it's not about winning and losing, but how you play the game. Well, for me, I've got to win." Coach DeMan preached the value of winning to the Forzanis and an entire generation of young Browns athletes. Forzani says that nobody goes into a serious endeavour to lose. As in life, the goal in football is to win and to keep winning.

Jordan Peterson, who grew up in Fairview, Alberta, believes, "Sports are a great analogy for life because life is like a game. Like sports, you are setting forth an aim and arranging your perceptions and actions to pursue that."

According to Tom, his older brother John put the Forzani business empire together. John's core values sounded like DeMan's at St. Francis: treat everyone with respect and emphasize teamwork. The Forzanis grew their business from one store to six hundred before selling the business for close to a billion dollars. Tom believed the business's power derived from concepts that good coaches preach daily.

Tom remarked, "It makes me sad to see kids leave sports without having had some success." As the receivers coach for the perennial champion Cochrane Cobras, Tom understands administrators' important role in supporting coaches: "People running schools don't seem to appreciate what athletics can do for communities."

After playing football for only one year at St. Francis, Forzani followed in the steps of his older brothers at Utah State where he shattered school records in receiving. In his senior year, he had 85 catches for 1,166 yards and 8 touchdowns. Even more remarkable was that the St. Francis grad led the entire NCAA in catches that season and had twenty more than the next-highest receiver. Forzani quickly credited his QB Tony Adams, who played with Minnesota, Kansas City, and San Diego for five years in the NFL. Adams also played for two years with the Toronto Argonauts.

The NFL tries its best to ensure parity and competitiveness among its teams, yet the same handful of teams dominate year after year. The worst teams get the first pick in the annual draft of college players, and the best teams get to pick from a less talented group of players. The league also has a salary cap, so teams are on an equal footing. Key individuals in good settings dominate sports like business.

DINOS IN BUSINESS

At age twenty-four, former Brown Chris Lewis was recruited to Enmax to head a sales team. Much like Dennis Kadatz, Lewis faced a formidable challenge at a young age. Lewis led a group of forty salespeople and quickly realized that twenty percent of his sales team produced ninety-two percent of sales. His employees criticized

Lewis for "unfairly" compensating his group's "elite eight." Lewis responded by calling a meeting and speaking with the group about accountability. He refused to give in and told them people would be fired if they could not grow their sales. Not everyone had to be a star, but everybody needed to contribute and grind out results.

Today Lewis uses the lessons that DeMan and Connellan taught in his work as a consultant for emerging businesses. "When I build companies, we start with having a good product and then I immediately move to people and build teams. Mature managers must be taught that you don't build teams where everyone is like you. Not everyone can be a star. You need grinders, but no one is above the team ever! My experiences in the pros paled compared to the Browns and Dinos. I'm so glad I stayed home to play with the Dinos!"

Lewis incorporated two other core principles of Dinos football when he applied accountability and optimism to his business leader and sports enthusiast roles. For Lewis, these concepts were ingrained in the Alberta economy. In a discussion about the Alberta economy in 2022, Lewis was unapologetic about his praise for the innovation and hard work of the oil and gas entrepreneurs who built the province. The overlap between sports success and business success was everywhere for Lewis.

Lewis sounded much like the Dinos coaching staff in 1983 who preached a brighter future despite the odds. "Let's take responsibility for our future instead of waiting for the next big thing," Lewis said. "Our city didn't have the nerve to go for the 2026 Olympics. The last one put us in great shape for thirty years: community service, volunteerism, etcetera. We built facilities and created a legacy."

As president of Snowboarding Alberta, Chris Lewis is passionate about making winter sports more inclusive. He hopes to attract recent immigrants to winter sports to make it affordable and fun for the participants, as sport is essential for any community. One community Lewis has targeted for growth in numbers is First Nations youth. Lewis became emotional when he described how First Nations youth desperately need winter sports, as mental illness and substance abuse rise exponentially during the winter on reserves.

All sports face a similar problem, with eighty percent of females leaving athletics by age fifteen. Lewis points to that statistic as another example of where sport must be better. The inclusivity that Lewis pursues is grounded in the notion that competition builds character and provides the requisite life skills. After the initial levels, Lewis believes the goal is to teach athletes how to compete. "We should recognize participation, but it's okay to celebrate winning. Those experiences are what we learn from. Don't cry when you lose—go home and learn how to improve. Sounds harsh, but the Canadian Olympic program has poured a ton of money into long-term athletic development." The world is competitive, and athletics is an excellent place to learn how to cope with life's ups and downs.

DINOS AND HIGGINS' MENTOR LOU HOLTZ

Competition drives leaders to give their employees or players an edge. Just as Connellan used Darrell Royal as a resource in making his high school offence, the 1980s Dinos sought help wherever they could. Notre Dame's national champion coach Lou Holtz profoundly affected Calgary's program. Not only did they have one of Holtz's former players, Tom Higgins, on the coaching staff, they also used the core of Holtz's player evaluation with the Dinos. Fasano said, "I always thought if you could learn one thing from a guy, it was worth an hour of my time. Even late in my career, I could go to a clinic and write twenty-five to thirty pages down."

Higgins was deeply impressed with the common sense and simplicity used by Connellan and Holtz regarding team rules. Holtz's two laws were: do the right thing and treat everyone you meet with dignity and respect. Then people can trust you. Holtz felt that his athletes intrinsically knew how to act; they should not be in the program if they didn't. Higgins used a similar philosophy with his CFL teams and extended it to include profanity. In Tom's words, "The use of profanity doesn't reflect well on the player, their families, or the organization, so I discouraged it through a curse jar that players would put a loonie in when they swore. It reminded the players that it was wrong." Higgins received two Annis Stukus Awards as CFL Coach of the Year and was a two-time winner of the Grey Cup (one as an assistant and one as the head coach). In addition to the Grey Cups, Higgins has fond memories of his role as a defensive line coach with the 1983 Vanier Cup-winning Dinos. Discipline gave Higgins' teams a competitive edge.

CONNELLAN'S VISION

In 1983 Connellan returned to the Dinos as the head coach. As Keith Holliday recalls, Connellan's mission was to get to Toronto and bring home the Vanier Cup. An earlier loss to University of Alberta alum Darwin Semotiuk's Western Ontario Mustangs in 1977 weighed heavily on Connellan and his staff. Connellan's staff in 1983 returned from 1977 and were on board with his mantra of returning to Toronto. Holliday remembers thinking, *We didn't even make the playoffs last season. What are we doing talking about going to Toronto?* They started talking about it at the beginning of two-a-days and kept it going all season. Connellan said, "You don't start getting ready for Toronto in November. It starts at the beginning of the season."

The start of the 1983 season could not have gone worse for the Dinos. Holliday recalls losing to the Dinos alumni in their annual match-up. The Dinos were crushed by the fact that the alum had not gone through two-a-days, much less any serious practising. The alumni continued their winning ways against Connellan's teams through 1986.

The following week, the Dinos travelled to Butte to play Montana Tech in a second exhibition game and outplayed them but failed to win. After a game in Saskatchewan, where they were beaten for a third time, the Dinos went on the road to Vancouver. The Thunderbirds, led by former Eskimo Frank Smith, was a strong program, and the game was close. Players still felt they had a chance even if they were winless. After the UBC game, the Dinos didn't lose until the end of 1984.

THOSE FABULOUS ASSISTANTS

Linebacker Keith Holliday attributes much of the Dinos' success to the men Connellan brought into the program as assistant coaches. On defence, Connellan hired Tom Higgins and Cam Innes. Holliday was duly impressed, calling Higgins "the best coach I had ever played for."

On the other side of the ball, Holliday recalled a fantastic group of coaches led by offensive coordinator Shane Wiley. "Wiley was calling plays with something in mind three or four plays down the road. Always setting up the other team to make a mistake. He was like a chess master." Shane Wiley, Rick Coleman, and Randy Berg were the other offensive coaches, and they were all on Connellan's 1977 team, which came close to a trip to the Vanier.

Mike Newans recalls the impact of offensive line coach Rick Coleman in particular. Coleman was a former Dino known for his intensity and uncompromising approach to line play and winning. His temper when the team was floundering was legendary. After one mediocre performance, two unfortunate Dinos were late getting on the bus and caught having a smoke by Coleman who proceeded to extinguish the cigarettes with his hand as he said, "I'm sick of this smoking crap!"

Once after a game in Butte, Montana where the Dinos came up short on the scoreboard, a dust-up occurred at a local saloon after some of the players took exception to comments made by locals. Fearing it might become an international incident, Coleman loaded the highly agitated players onto their buses and got them to safety north of the 49th parallel.

The commitment of those coaches scared Holliday off coaching when his playing days ended. Holliday remembers the coaches staying at the dorm, eating pizza, and watching films during training camp and was worried he could not make the same commitment. The coaches aimed to get to Toronto and bring the Vanier Cup back to Alberta, which required sacrifices from the assistants.

Former Dinos are quick to highlight the duality of Connellan's nature. "He's a character who knows how to work a room. But when he's serious, it's intense. Everyone listens because he means business," says Keith Holliday. "Everyone saw him as a great coach, but I saw him as a great coach and manager. He brought great people in and let them do their jobs," adds Chris Lewis.

The former principal from Viscount, Connellan was clearly in charge of those teams and had no difficulty sitting a player down and making a difficult call. Yet, Connellan possessed an intelligence that allowed him to find the humour in situations and apply it when needed. An example of Connellan's lighter side was in evidence at a coaches' conference hosted by the U of C in 1984. Coaches from across Alberta heard a talk by Connellan in which he revealed the approach the Dinos' coaching staff was taking to repeat the success of the 1983 season. He seemed to adjust the sound as he handed the microphone to the next speaker, his counterpart at the U of A. As Coach Donlevy began to speak, the feedback that erupted from the sound system was reminiscent of Jimi Hendrix's rendition of "The Star-Spangled Banner" at the Monterey Pops Festival. One couldn't help but feel sorry for Coach Donlevy as he tried to make himself heard above the squealing feedback. From the back of the auditorium, Connellan emerged to save his counterpart. As he walked back up the stairs, he said, "Coaches, your boys may have a future, but it sure isn't at the U of A!" His remark received lots of laughter and even Donlevy smiled, thinking, *What a guy.*

The vocabulary and jargon surrounding football constantly changes as media pundits struggle to separate themselves from their peers by using new terms. The term "process" has come to the forefront recently to describe a business's habits and the daily practices of winning sports programs. Processes are the daily practices that coaches use to achieve their goals, and a quick study of them is necessary. Coach DeMan and Coach Connellan developed practices that reflected their personalities and beliefs around the sport.

k

THE DINOS PIPELINE

Connellan and DeMan developed a connection that served the Browns and the Dinos. According to the Dinos' information director Jack Neumann, "Gary's kids were fundamentally sound, and Pete knew it." Neumann was referring to the physical nature of the game, which usually means tackling, blocking, and conditioning, but equally important was the team approach to the game that the Browns possessed. The pipeline of running backs from St. Francis was remarkable. It started with Dan Diduck and continued with Spoletini, the Geremiahs, and Lewis.

Although perceived as a man of routines and discipline, DeMan had an independent streak that allowed him to do things his way and on his own terms. The process that DeMan and his assistants developed at the north side high school should be examined by coaches as a potential template for their programs. For many years, DeMan's record of 218 wins and 56 losses was the record for wins in Canadian football. The number of coaches that graduated from St. Francis speaks loudly to DeMan's methods.

The current principal of St. Francis, Luigi Fortini, described DeMan as strategically building a program. As department head of physical education, DeMan made sure that he taught grade ten boys phys ed so that he could identify the talent coming into the school to fill positions on his basketball and football teams. Other department members taught the highly coveted grade eleven and twelve classes. According to Fortini, boys coming into the school wanted DeMan's class, as it would give them a chance to impress him with their athleticism.

DEMAN'S UNIQUE PLAYBOOK

The Browns' playbook borrowed heavily from previous decades, but DeMan adjusted it to his school's demographics. Unlike the Raymond Comets, DeMan had the luxury of big athletes with a smattering of speed. By going back in time for their playbook, the Browns were viewed, interestingly enough, as "original thinkers."

The genius of the Browns' offensive and defensive systems will be dealt with in greater detail in a later chapter, but for now we will put their systems into perspective. The single wing of the 1940s, 1950s, and early 1960s was emulated and admired by DeMan for its uniqueness, as teams in Canada had long abandoned it. As previously mentioned, single wing offences were the forerunner of today's modern offences that utilize tremendous athletes at QB who can beat opponents by running an option-style system or passing the ball. The Eskimos offence of the 1950s when Jackie Parker was the triple-threat QB was an excellent example of single wing concepts in action. QBs in the single wing were not managers handing the ball off or dropping back to pass, but athletes expected to make plays by running, passing the ball, and making critical decisions on option plays.

According to a former Brown, the playbook was straightforward in DeMan's offence. Like Darrell Royal, former Eskimos and Longhorns coach, everyone had to know the point of attack. DeMan did not care if the defence knew where the ball was being run; he felt the play should work anyway. The running back's job was to hit the hole hard without dancing or reading blocks like in the zone-blocking techniques of today's offences. "Hit the seam and run. We just bashed and bashed. One year our fullback was two hundred and seventy pounds, but he ran well! We would pass the ball maybe five times a game." Chris Lewis remarked that some years the Browns' line was bigger than the junior Calgary Colts' line.

DeMan employed a form of psychological warfare on his opponents using his massive linemen. The Browns' linemen were the first players onto the field and made a point of entering the area by the opposition bench whenever possible. As the Browns' linemen thundered by the opposition, Coach DeMan hoped that the first impressions made by the Browns would be lasting.

On defence, DeMan's staff ran an old, seldom-used variation of an odd-man front. For many years the Browns ran a 3-3 with a rover as opposed to the traditional 3-4 or 5-4 that most teams run. The rover could line up anywhere he thought the offence might attack. Sometimes the coaches would give the rover predetermined places to align, but most of the time it was up to the rover where he would go. Again, like in the offence, DeMan went to unconventional places for his systems. By using schemes, offensively and defensively, different opponents would have to take an unusual amount of time to prepare for the Browns.

TOGETHER EVERYONE ACHIEVES MORE

Like the Dinos and the Comets, the Browns respected the top-to-bottom role everyone played in chasing victories. Chris Lewis said the Browns did not cut anyone based on ability. DeMan confirmed this and said that as long as players abided by the rules, they were welcome. Lewis recalled the roster sometimes exceeding seventy-five players. A problem with rosters of that size is keeping everyone comfortable with their role and a potential lack of playing time. DeMan kept morale high in several ways, but most impressive was how he used the scout team players he called the "Beavers."

The Beaver squad was instrumental in the Browns and Dinos' success. The Beavers were players who might never see the field in a regular game but ran the other team's offence and defence in practice. They wore uniforms with the other team's star players' numbers on them to be readily identifiable in the different sets the opponents would run. The Beavers took great pride in giving their team the best possible look at the opponent's plays and personnel. The Beavers would learn and execute the plays to the best of their ability. The epic football movie *Rudy* is an example of a player from Notre Dame who had little chance of ever playing but who did his utmost in every practice to improve his teammates.

The psychological effect of having everyone on a team contributing is immeasurable. The happier and more purposeful locker rooms are free of selfishness and resentment. Another "team killing" behaviour on dysfunctional teams is the refusal of players to take responsibility for their actions and to blame others instead. Great teams share the pain of losses and the joy of victories.

Tom Forzani felt Coach DeMan understood the psychological makeup of the adolescent male better than anyone. For most males, adolescence lends itself well to DeMan's approach to the game. Browns players marvelled at DeMan's discipline and structured approach to life. One former Dino insisted his routines were so fixed that he ate the same sandwich daily. His approach to his football seemed predictable, yet trick plays and formations were encouraged by DeMan to keep the game fun for the boys. DeMan's successor, Joe Stambene, kept the traditions alive, and the legendary potluck banquets and awards nights are still alive and well.

Gary DeMan and Dennis Kadatz knew how to build teams, and one cannot help but think that the postwar era had something to do with that. Canada's sacrifices in defeating the Axis powers made an impression on those who lived through it—or who knew those who served overseas or at home. People knew the liberties they enjoyed came with a responsibility to uphold the values that served as the foundation of Canadian society. The recollections of players on the Browns, Dinos, and Huskies speak to an earlier era where the group mattered more than the individual. The pursuit of victory in WWII required a community to come together and sacrifice.

Building a competitive team or readying a society for war are different ventures, but loyalty and teamwork are everything in both situations. During WWII, communities pulled together and sacrificed. There was no other way to victory. The survival of democratic values was at stake. In sports, the stakes aren't as high, but the aim is the same—victory. A collective spirit and strenuous efforts are the expectation in any important endeavour.

Easily forgotten are the sacrifices made during WWII on the home front. The drama of battle scenes is hard for historians to compete with, but everyone had a role to play if the enemy was to be defeated. From the women thrust into dual roles in industry and as homemakers to children who missed their fathers to the planting of victory gardens to help supply the troops with food, the war touched everyone. The WWII "roster" included millions more than just the soldiers. The loss of loved ones and the crippling nature of the injuries suffered by veterans left marks that were hard to erase. Men and women born in the 1930s made countless sacrifices that benefitted the community.

Defeating the fascist powers in 1945 brought euphoria to the victorious nations. As the reality of Hitler's "Final Solution" unfolded, the mood changed to disgust and disbelief. The emerging Cold War and the threat of nuclear war lay like a heavy blanket over the postwar euphoria. Communities found an outlet for the joy they missed during WWII and during the Cold War in the rise of college and professional sports in the late 1940s and 1950s. In this historical setting, young coaches like Lombardi, Connellan, Dudley, DeMan, and Kadatz lived and developed into leaders.

THE HUSKIES' PACK LEADERS

In the national final on November 26, 1962, the *Edmonton Journal's* Hal Pawson must have made the hair stand up on the back of the necks of his readers when he wrote:

> My hat's off to Tony Rankel, Clarence Kachman and the others on the Huskies fine, little offence. But whenever I recall Edmonton's first-ever national junior football championship, I'll recall with awe Bobby Bateman's Bandits, the Huskies defence. In the first 50 minutes, they had done everything a defence could do against the Leafs and had virtually wrecked Montreal's great passing attack with interceptions. They had hammered themselves to near exhaustion against the bigger opposition. But for them, the game hadn't started. The real war came in the last 10 minutes. I lost track of how many times they had to stop the Leafs to win—and did. Each time I believed another stand was physically impossible, regardless of how indomitable Huskies' spirit might be. Common sense said that it had to yield, but what does common sense have to do with a team that doesn't know it was beaten?

The young men Hal Pawson mentioned in his article were the same fellows highlighted sixty years later by former teammates and opponents as the "lead sled dogs." Marv Roberts, a lineman with those championship teams, was complimentary of Rankel's leadership but not his golf game. "On the field, Rankel was way ahead of his time, ordering guys to go there or be there. He was in charge on the field, as he knew what everybody was supposed to do and how they should do it. Tony could throw a great spiral and had the respect of his teammates."

George Spanach was a good friend of Rankel's and knew the troubled background he grew up in. He appreciated his QB's leadership style. Rankel confided to Spanach many years later that he endured many hardships being raised by a single mother in the 1950s. Rankel came by his resiliency and toughness naturally.

Only one dog barked in the Huskies huddle, and that was Rankel. Spanach recalled one vintage "Rankel moment" during a game in Calgary when a defensive tackle stuffed a Huskies running back for no gain. The large Calgary defensive tackle, who hadn't missed many meals in his lifetime, mocked the Huskies for even trying to run a play in his vicinity. Rankel had had enough of the big man's chirping and asked him if he liked that play so much, would he like to see it again? Sure enough, Rankel went into the huddle and called the same play. Warren Hansen was the offensive lineman opposite the big Calgary player. He remembered looking at Rankel in disbelief but said nothing. The play was run and netted a first down. As the big man from Calgary dusted himself off, he was much quieter, but that didn't stop Rankel from calling the same play again, with a similar result. For Rankel, it was personal, and his teammates loved that side of him.

The inhabitants of Huskies House in the 1960s had little time for mediocrity. Like DeMan's St. Francis Browns, what players did on and off the field mattered equally. When the Southside Oilers transitioned to the Edmonton Huskies in the mid-1950s, the Huskies' first head coach, Murray Smith, set the tone for a generation of Edmonton coaches.

According to a long-term faculty co-worker at the University of Alberta, Dr. Gary Smith, Murray Smith was optimistic and a great communicator. Later, as a head coach at the University of Alberta, Smith put captains like Maynard Vollan, an engineering student, front and centre as team leaders. The student-athlete was very important to Dr. Smith, as it was to DeMan. Dr. Smith states, "It wasn't cool to be mediocre in the classroom."

Great coaching doesn't just happen. It must be learned and implemented. The example that Smith set for his players, which included his captain, Dennis Kadatz, was characterized by a strong belief in fundamentals and work ethic. The expectations for players and coaches were high but not aggressive or humiliating, as he respected his players. Smith believed that such an approach would give the Huskies the best chance to fulfill their promise to produce good citizens.

CURLING'S ASPIRATIONS FOR INTERNATIONAL RECOGNITION AND THE HUSKIES

The later championship Huskies teams were remembered by many as a great collection of clean-cut young men dressed in shirts and ties. Marv Roberts remembers going to Pickles Men's Wear on the corner of 101ˢᵗ Street and Jasper Avenue to get a blazer with a crest. Pickles was one of the early directors, along with Shipka, Bateman, and Henderson, who created the first Huskies team of 1954. Mark Twain put it this way: "A policeman in plain clothes is a man; in uniform, he is ten. Clothes and title are the most potent thing, the most formidable influence, in the universe. They move the human race to willing and spontaneous respect for the judge, the general, the admiral, the bishop, the ambassador, the frivolous earl, the idiot, the duke, the sultan, the king, the emperor. No great title is efficient without clothes to support it."

Coaches Smith and Kadatz may have never read the above passage, but they sure embraced and hammered home the importance of standards for team attire. Little did Smith and Kadatz know that their insistence on a uniform appearance for the Edmonton Huskies Football Club would play a massive role in helping former Huskies player Warren Hansen transform the game of curling from a popular pastime to a professional Olympic sport popular around the world.

Hansen came to the Huskies from just north of Edmonton and had a background like many others on the Wildcats and the Huskies. Hansen's parents were first-generation Canadians who emigrated from Denmark. Like many of his generation, Hansen was no stranger to hard work, owing to his mixed-farming background. Second-generation Canadians often left their parents scratching their heads at their sons' and daughters' decisions to forgo working eighteen-hour days to have fun playing games.

Hansen's farm boy determination to make the Huskies later found its way to the curling rink, where he won a Brier with the Hec Gervais rink in 1974. After his curling career ended, he served as event director for Curling Canada and retired in 2015. Warren was primarily responsible for moving major curling events into hockey arenas, implementing dress codes, and bringing in officiating for significant events. The inclusion of curling as a demonstration sport in the 1988 Calgary Olympics was largely because of the dedication of Hansen and his counterpart in Calgary, Ray Kingsmith.

A HUSKIE TAKES CURLING TO THE OLYMPICS

Curling culture takes great pride in the game that epitomizes Canada and what Canadians think of themselves. Our geography and climate, like most nations, define us to a large degree. Curling helped get people out of their houses and into clubs that promoted fun, friendship, and good-natured competition. The short days and the long nights of winter posed a challenge for Canadians interested in maintaining their sanity. Curling was unique in that couples could participate together on a friendly basis, and those wishing for a more intense atmosphere could enter their province's play-downs to win the right to represent their community in the national championship—the Brier. The Canadian curling establishment had long embraced the social aspects of curling, which included smoking and drinking while playing. For the game to be treated as a sport, Hansen knew the game had to advance to a more professional version.

The struggle between Hansen, as a representative of the Canadian Curling Association, and Ed Werenich was hardly a struggle, according to Hansen. "It wasn't a fight; it was a war!" Werenich's ten Brier appearances representing Ontario and two world championship victories endeared him to Canadians. Unfortunately, Werenich's persona and waistline detracted from European views of what an Olympic sport and an Olympic athlete should look like.

In 1987, the Canadian Curling Association told Werenich he had to lose eighteen pounds or he would be disqualified. The decision by Hansen and the CCA did not endear him to Canadians who had long sought relief from winter in national favourites like Kraft Dinner, chicken wings, pizza, and beer. To this day, "the Wrench" is still a folk hero to the Canadians who followed the fight between him and the CCA. Still, Hansen refused to bow to public pressure and eventually got international support to accept curlers as athletes and the game as an Olympic sport. Like his old coach, Kadatz, Hansen was singular in his focus. Curling was a great game and deserved Olympic status. Nothing would deter him. Hansen's legacy is seen most winter nights on television. It was worth the fight.

Coaches Winkles of ASU, Kadatz and Smith of the Huskies, Connellan of the Dinos, Dudley of the Comets, and Ivy of the Eskimos would have endorsed Hansen's war with the "old boys of curling." Dinos from the 1980s still marvel at Mike Newans' intensity and weekly battle to put "his guys" in the best light with the best uniforms in the league. Like Newans, Brian Dudley's wife, Diane, went to great lengths to ensure the Comets would inspire respect. She still remembers the detergent that gave the Comets' uniforms their shiny appearance. Good teams learn to take nothing for granted regarding their appearance and the pride they share in their oneness.

UNIFORMITY AND WINNING

Competition is about winning. When Bob Dean's teams ran onto the field, opponents marvelled at their uniformity and cohesion. The Vic boys believed and benefitted from the idea that their look intimidated opponents. A ragtag group of athletes in uniforms that do not match present themselves in a negative light, which competitors subconsciously or consciously use to their advantage. Dean's military background may have had something to do with the carefully choreographed warm-up and attention to detail. Opponents weren't playing individuals when they played Victoria; they were playing a team with a collective spirit and look.

Jack Rutherford was neither an Edmonton Huskie nor an Eskimo in the early 1950s. Still, as a prominent sportsman on the Alberta sports scene, he was very familiar with the methods employed by those teams to achieve what they did. A veteran of some great Wildcats teams from the 1950s (then known as the Maple Leafs), Jack had considerable experience as an athlete. His competitive drive was unmatched in increasing market share in multi-million-dollar companies. The former Edmonton Wildcat player and manager recalled being named the Edmonton Molson sales manager, and his first job was in his words "to build a team—sound familiar?" His first hire was Brian Dickinson, a Wildcats alum who played offensive line and then coached in the 1960s.

Marv Roberts, an integral part of three national championship teams with the Huskies, was the second man hired by Rutherford. Jack described Marv as a big, wonderful guy with lots of presence. Appearances and a team attitude mattered for Rutherford. Jack laughed when he reminisced that Roberts had a much longer career with Molson than he did.

Jack repeatedly sought disciplined employees, and he drove them to be their best within a team concept. Rutherford embraced Twain's mantra. Shoes had to be shined, cars had to be clean, and employees had to be sharply dressed if they wanted to work for Canada's biggest beer company. Brian Dickinson laughingly recalled that even a short visit to the office without a tie could find an employee going home to put one on.

When Connellan and his staff decided to think big in 1983 (the staff's first year) to win the Vanier Cup, they raised more than just a few eyebrows. Rutherford would have wholeheartedly endorsed Connellan's vision, as it is imperative in business and sports to think big. "You have to be thinking of the next level. Bake sales aren't going to do it." Rutherford was on the management team in 1981, responsible for putting the plan together for Lotto 649. The sales strategy went from having charitable groups in malls selling them to online terminals in retail operations. Actual competitors, in whatever field, leave no stone unturned in getting an advantage.

THE CULTURE OF COMPETITION

The competitive nature of many Eskimos found an outlet in coaching after their playing days were over. Games between old teammates were intense and personal. Maybe it was the pain of losing marathon games of gin rummy or the locker room antics of their playing days, but old resentments were played out on Friday nights between the Saints, Lancers, T Birds, Redmen, and Lords. Bo Jereniuk remembers one time as Coach Dean and he were leaving Coronation Park after a game, Coach Johnny Bright was walking into the stadium. After a brief exchange of pleasantries, rather than wishing Bright good luck, Bob ended the conversation with, "I hope you lose." Dean never turned around to check Bright's reaction, but Jereniuk did. He recalled, "It was personal, but they always went for beers; they got along."

Several decades after the Eskimos won three Grey Cups, former Dinos and Stamps coach Tom Higgins observed a difference in how Edmonton and other CFL franchises operated. Tom Higgins was a two-time Coach of the Year winner in the CFL and knew how to achieve success. "Any team with success is built on a foundation of culture. You must find the people who buy into that culture. Culture, whatever it is, comes down to having people that unselfishly play for each other. You must look for good people to bring in—that was the key to the Eskimos."

The pursuit of perfection united the brightest football lights in the starry skies of Alberta's sports history. The similarities in their philosophies and practices were striking and rooted in their desire to fulfill their mission. There was nothing special about the types of plays they ran, as other teams had similar playbooks. What separated them from their opponents was how they mastered their systems and standards to achieve a sense of true team. The leaders in these programs travelled different paths, but they all had the advantage of their colleagues, mentors, and families' support and wisdom to fuel their competitive advantage. Alberta was made better by their relentless pursuit of glory.

CONNELLAN'S FORMULA FOR ACCOUNTABILITY

Each person and program highlighted in this book was different from the programs and people they competed against. Connellan in particular can only be understood by closely examining how he achieved such a high level of accountability for himself, his coaches, his players, and his support staff. In Connellan's own words, he was constantly "throwing papers" at his people in the form of evaluations. Players evaluated coaches, coaches evaluated players, players evaluated themselves, and everyone assessed the program.

The players were also asked to submit weekly timetables for studying and training. The kinds of evaluations that Connellan asked of everyone were evidence of his belief in people's ability to be reflective and learn from their successes and failures. The goal of the process was to win more football games, but the reflection and honesty required was a life lesson that could be used upon graduation. Many coaches would be reluctant to open themselves to criticism, but the 1980s Dinos used it to get better and win championships. The phrase "go to the mirror" is often used in our society, but it is rarely practised. People avoid their shortcomings by avoiding the mirror, but not the Dinos players, coaches, and support staff.

University coaches have the luxury of time over their high school counterparts. With limited time in the classroom, college coaches can focus on their program's details. The following pages detail the unique processes Connellan employed to bring accountability to the program. The questions on the evaluations that Connellan generated were sensitive, honest, and to the point. Their willingness to be open to evaluation, reflection, and accountability made the Dinos champions. The Alberta taxpayers got their money's worth from Connellan.

All coaches like to think their players and staff are accountable. Usually, it's the scoreboard they are talking about. The former Viscount Bennett principal turned head coach pulled no punches in the meetings that followed these evaluations and was as likely to reprimand players and assistant coaches who underrated themselves as knock the cockiness out of players who overrated their contributions.

"Know thyself" was one of Socrates's main contributions to Greek philosophy, but this saying has often been interpreted incorrectly. Rather than looking inward, as many believe Socrates was implying, it meant to look honestly at one's place in the community. Excessive pride and ego had no place in Socrates's community. The same is true for those who undervalue their contributions. Connellan's talks with players were a chance to establish responsibility for themselves and others associated with the team.

In addition to accountability, Connellan paid attention to the details he could control, leading to victories and championships. This included the responsibilities of coaches on game day. Connellan emphasized information gathering and a positive, solution-based approach to communication between everyone on game day. The spotter's box could only send information to the field coaches in the second quarter. They were to check that the opposing team's lineups were what they expected and that they ran the schemes they had been practising against that week. At halftime, it was expected that the coaches from the box would relay what defensive fronts the opponent was running on first and second downs. They would also recommend what run and pass plays should be run and any trick plays that might be effective.

Players also had a job to do in gathering information during a game. It was expected that they would be able to identify who was responsible for picking them up in coverage and where the safety was located. They also had to assess who the weakest tackles, defensive ends, corners, and halfbacks were. Information from the players would be instrumental in calling plays in the second half, giving the Dinos the best chance of success in the second half.

Specific jobs were also doled out to bench personnel. Two coaches were responsible for bench control—one on defence and one on offence. The backup QB recorded the prescribed information, and the starting QB was to remain with the head coach. Recorded information included which receiver caught the pass, which player got penalized, how long the punt was, and how long the run back was. Length of possession and score were also recorded by the backup QB. Training staff and equipment managers had prescribed roles and were forever busy. Focus, accountability, and a positive attitude were crucial on game day, as they were every day. The acronym TEAM (together everybody achieves more) was more than a cliché for the Dinos.

Injured players were strongly encouraged to remain active and involved. Injured players were defined as anyone who was unable to condition or who was injured in the game. During the season, all players were to report to the physio at the appointed time unless excused by the head trainer, head coach, or defensive coordinator. Missed appointments cost players five dollars for the first miss and ten dollars for the second transgression. Players who missed appointments were also given jobs to do.

Athletes who were hurt were not given a free pass to miss practices, spend leisurely time in hot tubs, get rub downs, or hang out. All injured players were to attend practice. They were even told what to wear: sweats and a helmet. Their jobs included helping the managers move bags in and out of the equipment shed. Injured players were not excused from conditioning. If they could not run, they were expected to do an alternative activity. When players returned from an injury, they were expected to be in shape and to contribute. These expectations were given to the players on a single piece of paper.

Coaches of particular units also had their football lives detailed for the season on a single piece of paper. Before the season, the coaches met and agreed on the skills the players in their units would be drilled on. The coach's sheet for the offensive line is interesting in that not only are the drills listed, but so are ways to ensure a positive and enthusiastic atmosphere. Short-yardage drills featured the first unit against the defence's first and second teams. The offensive line would always be challenged by the first-team defence but was expected to feel the success against the second team. The coach's sheet says in brackets that after competitive team drills, clapping and enthusiasm were expected as it was being run. Connellan left nothing to chance.

On the coach's sheet, the offensive lineman was also expected to understand the plays and why and how they were designed. Shades of the old Eskimos split-T principles were evident as well. Offensive linemen were told to take splits as wide as possible while protecting their inside gaps. They were also told to be patient on specific plays to let the defensive players take themselves out of the play. Counters and bootlegs were plays where it was essential for the lineman not to be overly aggressive. The sheets the coaches assembled for their units were easy enough for most coaches at the high school level to understand.

The evidence of Connellan's concern for the players fulfilling their academic and athletic potential was the weekly schedule he asked them to fill out in September and January. The fall and winter schedules had hourly boxes from 8:00 a.m. till 11:00 p.m. that the athletes had to indicate with a "WL" when they would weight lift, "WORK" when they were at a job, proposed study times, classes being taken, and the times. In bold, capital letters on the sheet, Connellan impressed on the players, **"DO NOT USE FOOTBALL AS AN EXCUSE FOR ACADEMICS, AND DO NOT USE ACADEMICS AS AN EXCUSE FOR FOOTBALL."**

Team goals were at the top of the timetable sheet and were simple and to the point: "To win the Vanier Cup, to improve every week as a team and as individuals, and to succeed academically." A reminder of the Dinos commitment to academics was that all first-year players and those on academic probation had to attend study hall every Monday night. Veteran players served as academic captains and provided assistance and guidance when needed.

The requirements for training were explicit—three points essential to team success: commitment and responsibility, will to prepare, and communication. To facilitate readiness, players were not to hold jobs in the fall and could only commit to employment for up to two days a week during the winter months. Exceptions to the winter work rules could be made only in consultation with the head coach.

CONNELLAN'S QUESTIONNAIRES

Alberta's pulp and paper industry should have sponsored the 1980s Dinos, as yet another sheet was distributed for expectations regarding the players' analysis of film during the season. Players were expected to analyze film and not use it for entertainment purposes. Players travelling with the team watched film two to three times per week, and those not playing once per week. Players who saw something interesting about their opponents would submit a scouting report to their coach. Viewing film as a group was encouraged, as team members could reflect and learn from each other. Dinos staff expected peer support and leadership.

Another demand on players was that they would honestly appraise the program. The confidence and strength of the staff lay in its commitment to be better, and the players were given an important voice in this regard. Communication was essential to let everyone know where strengths and weaknesses lay and where the program might need to improve.

The categories on the player year-end questionnaire sheet were interesting in terms of their order. Up first was the coaching section. Each question had a box to tick that would allow a score to be assigned for that area. Players were asked if their coaches gave them the necessary techniques appropriate for game conditions. They were also asked to rate their coaches on their willingness to challenge them to be better and how to improve. In an interesting twist, the players were asked if they were told what they did well and if they were allowed to give input and discuss their concerns. Similar questions were asked in the second section, which dealt with practice organization. The first two sections focused on areas the coaches had direct control over.

The third category dealt with the attitude and morale of the players and the team. This section had half as many questions as the other two sections, but they cut to the heart of what constitutes a team. The first two questions were: "Do you feel close to your teammates?" and "Did your teammates assist you in becoming a better player?" The third question dealt with the team's overall morale. The last question was squarely on the coaches, as it asked: "Were you treated fairly by your coaches?" Academics was the fourth category, and it put more of the responsibility on the players to reveal what they devoted to their studies.

At the top of the year-end questionnaire, players were asked to help recruit potential Dinos, players, and managers. The team was the community, and the players owed the community their best. That included responsibility for continuing the local recruitment of athletes. Player efforts and input were valued and considered, but the last word always belonged to the vision of the athletic department and coaching staff, headed by Peter Connellan.

The first of four essential sections asked about the relationship between the offensive and defensive units. The direct nature of the questions is startling. The questions were in the form of statements, and the players would either agree or disagree on a scale of 1–5. To give you a sense of the seriousness of the questionnaire, here are the statements.

1. We cooperate well with the defensive unit.
2. We communicate well with the defensive unit.
3. We see the defensive unit as maintaining a winning attitude.
4. The defensive unit gets the recognition it deserves.
5. The defensive unit seems to give 100%.
6. We are proud of our defensive unit.

7. The defensive unit is effective.
8. We treat the defensive unit with respect.
9. We understand the game plan of the defence.
10. We understand the strengths and weaknesses of the defence.

The questions the Dinos coaching staff asked of the players and asked of the position coaches were equally blunt, but they give us insights into what Connellan expected of his coaches. This section focused on the communication and personal skills of the assistant coaches. Connellan revealed his emphasis on sound instructional practices coupled with coaches who cared about their athletes. The statements speak volumes and need little elaboration.

1. Our position coach gets along well with our coordinator.
2. My position coach gives helpful advice.
3. I respect our position coach.
4. I get accurate feedback on my performance.
5. My position coach is available when I need him.
6. My position coach wants me to be successful.
7. I can talk to my position coach about personal problems.
8. My position coach gives positive feedback.
9. The strength and conditioning coach is helpful.
10. The athletic trainers are helpful.

At the end of the year, players would meet with the coaches and discuss their player evaluation sheets. The headings and categories were as direct and to the point as their evaluations of the coaches and programs. There were eleven categories in which athletes would be evaluated, and there was also a chance to self-reflect on how players viewed themselves in those areas. Eighty points were possible, and some categories were weighted more heavily than others. The player evaluation sheet was heavily influenced by the format the University of Notre Dame used the year they won their national championship under Lou Holtz.

It is essential to go into some detail on the player evaluations to show the athletes what mattered and how the coaches viewed them. You cannot expect athletes to be accountable unless they know what they should aim for. The eleven categories were: competition, skill level, mental preparedness, intensity, commitment and work habits, durability, coachability, off-field discipline, character, and performance role. A player's point totals would be compared with the coaches at the meeting to ensure everyone was straight on what was good and what needed improvement. The position coach, coordinator, and head coach would all have a say.

Before we get to the most insightful questionnaires, we must clarify the difficulties in creating a unified, determined group out of dozens of individuals. The obvious groups within a team are the defence, offence, and special teams. Football may be the only game where those three groups are separate and sit on the bench and watch their teammates defend, attack, or be on special teams. If you are an offensive player, you watch your defenders fight, scratch, and claw to keep your opponents out of your end zone. While they play, the other groups cheer, hope, and pray their mates do their job. It sounds easy, and it is as long as you are winning.

Even if the team is doing well, many problems can creep in. As mentioned earlier, the 1980s Oilers had a problem with jealousy and resentment around who was getting the credit for wins. Competition between teammates for recognition can quickly become a problem. Dr. Smith's background in football would have been a great help in turning the Oilers around. It is common in football to have athletes who forget that they got into the endzone with the help of eleven teammates. They need to be reminded that it is a collective effort. Skilled players who appreciate their teammates get more effort from them. The unsung heroes in contact sports who spend the entire game engaged in hand-to-hand combat appreciate the odd pat on the back.

A team's backbone is tested most when things are not going well. The best teams embrace the notion that together everybody achieves more. Let us play out a typical scenario. A QB goes back to pass, the receiver runs ten yards, heads to the sideline, turns, and sprints straight down the field. The QB fakes a pass when the receiver runs to the sideline, pulls the ball, waits for him to go downfield, and launches a fifty-yard pass for a touchdown. An uneducated viewer blames the poor coverage of the defensive back. A more knowledge-able observer wonders why there was not more pressure on the QB. On some teams, the defensive lineman would grumble about the terrible coverage of the defensive backs and, by doing so, not take responsibility for their part in the tragedy. The defensive backs would retaliate by saying they couldn't cover a receiver indefinitely. The defensive back's coach would tell everyone that he had warned his players about that play. On bad teams, the exit doors are overrun with people fleeing the "crime scene."

At first glance, defences look bad when the opponents score a lot of points. A casual observer sees the lopsided score and blames the players or the defensive coordinator's scheme. However, the truth can often be much more complicated. If the offence cannot generate many first downs and is punting the ball from deep in their end, the other team's offence will be starting in good field position. If an offence can generate first downs and consistently move the ball, the defence's job is much easier, they will be better rested, and the opponent will have a longer way to go to score. The same is true of a good kicking game. If a punter can boom punts deep into enemy territory, the defence has a much easier job defending, as the offence has a long way to go to score. If the offence and kicking game is weak, the defence has a much tougher job keeping the opponent from scoring.

Lastly, and probably the most challenging thing, is creating a cohesive group of coaches. Coaches are natural leaders with strong views on the game they love, and sometimes frustrations build and things are said. Sometimes a coach's body language betrays his feelings, and whatever the case, it can create doubt in the athletes. In the toughest of times, players look to their coaches for strength and potential solutions. On most football teams, coaches call every play, and this gives them an influence that is unmatched in sports.

Another problem that can cause massive dysfunction on the coaching staff is overly ambitious assistants who wish to unseat or prematurely take the head coach off their "throne." They may look for support from other assistants or, even more devastatingly, woo the players to their cause. The larger the staff, the greater the chance that this will occur. In losing programs, the problems are magnified.

Connellan was acutely aware of the internal problems that can befall teams. Opponents aren't the main culprit in stopping teams from reaching their potential. His background as an administrator of a high school was an excellent training ground for being a head coach, as school staff rooms and negative personalities are often obstacles in building a team.

This final questionnaire assigns grades to the players in specific categories that, taken together, paint a picture of where the athlete is and where he needs to go to get better.

<u>Dino Player Evaluation Scores</u>

Players could score 80 points and were categorized as follows:

Points	Team Category	Individual Category
58 - 65	Red – National Championship Calibre	All Canadian Calibre
50 - 58	Gold – Conference Championship Calibre	All Conference Calibre (starter)
45 - 50	White – Possible Conference Championship Calibre	Possible Traveller
Below 45	Grey – Poor Chance of Conference Championship Calibre	Not a starter or traveller

Circle the phrase that best describes the athlete based on this year's performance.

Competition: Will not be beaten – tenacity

Refuses to lose at anything	Loves to Compete	Good Competitor	Likes to Win if Convenient	Doesn't Matter
10	8	6	4	2

Skill Level: Athletic ability, consistency, techniques

All Canadian	All Conference	Start on winner	Can Contribute	Little Help
10-9	8-7	6-5	4-3	2-1

Mentally Prepared: Mental Errors, confidence level, confidence

Always Focused	Seldom Loses Focus	Gets Distracted	Excuses	Not Prepared
10-9	8-7-6	5-4	3-2	1

Intensity:

Great Hitter	Good Hitter	Average Hitter	Poor Hitter	Won't Hit
5	4	3	2	1

Commitment and Work Habits: ACADEMIC - Will to prepare

Whatever it Takes	Does the Extra Thing	What is Required	Does the Minimum; have to push	Does nothing
10-9	8-7-6	5-4	3-2	1-0

Commitment and Work Habits: Will to prepare (wt. training, physical prep) in season - out of season

Whatever it Takes	Does the Extra Thing	What is Required	Does the Minimum; have to push	Does nothing
10-9	8-7-6	5-4	3-2	1-0

Durability: Toughness

Never Gets Hurt	Sometimes Hurt	Can't Count on Him	Always Hurt
3	2	1	0

Coachability:

Takes coaching well	Does it	Does it easy way	Does it his way	Doesn't do it at all
4	3	2	1	0

Great instincts	Tell him once	Learns quickly	Learns with reps	Hard to teach
5	4	3	2	1

Off Field Discipline:

Team comes first	Follows all team rules	Likes to have a good time	Social life comes first
5	4	3	2-0

Character:

Outstanding character	Fine person	Some flaws	Questionable	Get rid of him (many flaws)
4	3	2	1	0

Performance Role: Positive vs Negative Force

Does his best	No complaints	Will not perform his role	Complainer
5-4	3-2	1	0

DEMAN'S UNUSUAL OFFENSE

Coach Gary DeMan of the Browns had many of the same beliefs about sport as Connellan. His ultimate goal was to produce individuals with values and an approach to competition that would serve the community. His emphasis on sportsmanship and personal accountability was striking, as he expected players and coaches to commit to his values.

DeMan was adept at giving his opponents a headache when presenting them with the unexpected. Trick plays and unique ways of running an offence or defence were a trademark of St. Francis football. DeMan explained it simply as wanting his opponents to prepare for a different type of team.

DeMan's wife, Sally, remembered how Gary, on his summer holidays, would spend hours floating around Lake Okanagan with his clipboard and pencil, fine-tuning his offences and defences. He looked for an edge and found it by returning to the single wing offence that featured an unbalanced line and a shotgun snap to the QB behind the guard. The single wing fell out of favour in the 1950s; therefore, coaches in the following decades had little knowledge of how to defend against it. Jim Whitelaw of Lethbridge Collegiate Institute had successfully run the single wing at the high school level, but only a few in Calgary had experience with LCI. The single wing would look a lot like some offences today that highlight great athletes at QB, but DeMan's offence was based on deception and timing. That has largely been lost in today's game.

One series in the Browns' offence was called the spinner, as the QB, upon receiving the snap, turned his back to the defence, who could not see the ball as running backs crisscrossed behind him. Someone eventually emerged with the ball, with the QB bootlegging out in the opposite direction. In DeMan's single wing offence, the line had more men on one side of the centre than the other. Sometimes the defence did not consider the unbalanced approach, which gave the Browns a numerical advantage. If the defence did not react, he ran a power sweep or reverse one the outmanned side of the defence. DeMan constantly made the opposing players and coaches respond to his team and their sets.

Surprising the defence was DeMan's favourite approach. In one offensive set, he took half the line and running backs, split them fifteen yards from the main body of the offence, and ran a series of plays. He could instead run to that side, throw a screen, or throw the ball downfield to them. DeMan's genius was running that set just before halftime, so the opponent would spend the intermission trying to figure out adjustments to what the Browns were doing. DeMan believed the set would not win games but might contribute by unsettling the opposition. Another twist DeMan used was to save this unusual tactic for the playoffs when it was too late for their opponents to devote practice time in preparation for it.

Yet another trick DeMan employed was running the QB in motion while under the centre. Sometimes the Browns ran out of the traditional T formation with the QB taking the snap directly from the centre. Coach DeMan had an excellent relationship with the refereeing community, as he felt they deserved respect like everyone else. DeMan knew defences rarely accounted for the QB going out for a pass, so he innocently asked a referee how to put his QB in motion from a position under centre. The referee responded that if the QB had his hands on the centre's back and not between his legs, it would be possible for him to go into motion before the snap. In one semifinal game against Bishop Grandin, the Browns executed the play perfectly with a pass thrown from a future Dino and CFL running back named J.P. Izquierdo. Years later, Izquierdo famously remarked on a CFL photo given to DeMan that he had been misplaced as an RB/receiver and should have been a QB.

Offensive line splits were crucial to how St. Francis approached their offensive game. The snap to the QB, who was five yards behind the line, made him vulnerable to any defenders who penetrated the backfield, so DeMan cut the splits to one to two feet to allow the QB time to execute his fakes. The tight splits allowed the Browns to take advantage of their traditionally huge offensive linemen, as they were allowed to move straight ahead rather than worry about the area between them and their linemates. Trapping with those big linemen was another favourite trick to give his teams an edge. By pulling his linemen and giving them an angle to attack an unsuspecting defensive player, he forced his opponents to practise techniques they weren't used to.

AND HIS DEFENCE WAS UNUSUAL

DeMan employed the same strategy on defence, as he designed a defence that nobody else would be familiar with. The defence was a traditional three-man front with defensive linemen covering the offensive centres and tackles. Stacked directly behind the defensive linemen were linebackers who often blitzed. This was a nightmare for offensive linemen. Like the single wing, the 3-3 stack forced the offence to prepare for a different opponent when they played the Browns. Many years later, Mike Leach popularized the defence at Texas Tech University and enjoyed tremendous success. When asked why he chose the 3-3 defence, Leach's response was the same as DeMan's in that he wanted a unique approach that required opponents to spend an inordinate amount of time preparing for.

Another aspect of the 3-3 defence that DeMan ran was his use of a rover. Reminiscent of the defence that the Pittsburgh Steelers ran several decades later, the Browns ran a rover free to call the defence and line up where he felt was most advantageous. Chris Lewis recalled the tremendous freedom he enjoyed in that position. He loved the 3-3 stack, as he could be a traditional linebacker or move into the secondary and play on the line. Troy Polamalu was the "Chris Lewis" of those great Steeler defences and must have had the same sentiments as Lewis.

As mentioned earlier, the Hill was used after games to remind players that things needed to improve. Players who received penalties were required to run the number of hills corresponding to the number of yards the infraction cost the team. A roughing penalty of fifteen yards cost the player fifteen hills. DeMan believed using the Hill for conditioning greatly strengthened his players' legs and increased their drive. Running after the game reminded the team that it was time to move on to the next game and put the last game to rest.

The Browns' singing prowess in no way matched their ability to play football, but it was an important tradition. The singing began after they were out of earshot of the stadium, and win or lose it was a part of the post-game ritual. When asked why the team sang after losses, DeMan, without hesitation, replied that it was to celebrate their effort, "and we were optimistic that we would defeat them in the playoffs." The message for the Browns was that they had not lost the game but had merely run out of time. The season was not over until the final whistle sounded.

YOU CAN'T DO IT ALONE

Coach DeMan's wife, Sally Williams, was a star Panda basketball player at the U of Alberta and highly sympathetic to a coach's drive for excellence. Gary had an essential ally in Sally, who appreciated the challenges of athletics. Sally was the team's centre when they won the Western Canadian Championships in 1958. Gary remembers visiting Sally in Irricana and finding out later that Sally's mother told her husband to take Sally somewhere when they knew Gary was coming. Sixty-three years later, the couple's defiance of Sally's parents proved correct, as they made a formidable team.

One of DeMan's favourite memories of the St. Francis Invitational Basketball Tournament was the social event he ran at his house just up the street from the school. Sally was in charge and made great spreads for the coaches and referees. Player leaders from all the teams were also invited but were contained downstairs. The tournament attracted teams from across Western Canada and the United States and was a massive hit. DeMan's inclusion of the referees in the festivities was in keeping with his respect for their work. Sally's patience, understanding, and support for the young men at St. Francis made great things possible. In Gary's estimation, none of it would have been possible without her.

One of the advantages that DeMan earned from the tournament and the social was his enduring friendships. CFL Hall of Famers Johnny Bright and Ron Lancaster coached at the tournament, and I am sure Bright in particular appreciated the efforts made by Sally and the other wives to put on a feast fit for a king. Superintendents often came to Calgary with their teams, especially those associated with the American teams. One connection DeMan made resulted in him being a featured speaker at a football conference in Texas. When asked how coaches in Texas received a Canadian football coach, DeMan smiled and said he was surprised by their attentiveness and interest in how he did things.

DUDLEY DIPPED INTO THE PAST

Approximately 280 kilometres south of Calgary, the founding father of Raymond football and the Southern Alberta High School Football League used similar strategies to ensure his teams had an edge. Coach Brian Dudley dominated the league with a system like DeMan's that drew upon the strengths of a bygone era.

Dudley used pulling guards to attack the perimeter of defences. Dudley picked big, athletic players who could run and block downfield to ensure success. Like many great offensive minds, including Vince Lombardi and Bear Bryant of Alabama, Dudley felt that it was crucial to run outside for good gains. Making big plays off the edge of the offensive line forced the defence to widen its alignment, opening up the middle. Also, an offence is hard-pressed in high school to have long drives of over ten plays. Rather than four to six yards per play, good offences must make several plays a game over fifteen yards if they are to succeed.

Running guards were a vital ingredient of the successful teams of the 1950s and their split-T offences. A name that fans of the CFL from the last century would recognize, Lloyd Fairbanks, is a part of Raymond folklore. His stature, well over 6 feet and 235 pounds, made him an imposing presence at guard running down the field, hunting down undersized defensive halfbacks. In Dudley's offence, the first guard to pull blocked out or sealed the first outside defender. The second pulling guard ran past the end man and then turned upfield to lead the running back. The guards needed to pull quickly and in a straight line to the point of attack. Fairbanks was a tremendous athlete, and in the Raymond tradition, he also played basketball. Dudley reinforced the importance of his pulling guards with frequent player of the game awards.

Southern Alberta's high winds are tough on offensive coordinators. Dudley's emphasis on attacking the perimeter of the defence limited him to handing the ball off instead of using the traditional pitch or option football of the split-T series. The Eskimos of the 1950s would have been a much different club if they had been located south of Calgary on the eastern slopes of the Rockies. Dudley's sweep to the outside was done with a hand-off, much like Vince Lombardi made famous with his Green Bay sweep in the 1960s. The pulling guards on most plays made Dudley's attack predictable, but defences could not cheat because of the counters he ran against the flow of the defence. Another way he took advantage of overly aggressive defences was to fake the run and pass the ball. Dudley only used the pass eight to ten times per game but found the play-action pass to be very effective.

Another way that the early Comets were unusual was Dudley's use of the quick kick. Again, this was an adaptation made because of the fierce winds that would whip across the high plains of southern Alberta. The quick kick, which is hardly seen anymore, is a play where the offence punts the ball on the first or second down rather than waiting for the third one. Usually, the kick is executed by tossing the ball back from the QB to a running back who is good at kicking and then punting the ball over the unsuspecting defence. Many offences used the quick kick during the 1950s and 1960s when ball control and field position were more important. Dudley recalled that he viewed the quick kick as an easy way to gain ground when the wind was sometimes seventy kilometres an hour at the back of the offence. The threat of the quick kick forced the secondary of the defence to back off the line of scrimmage, making them less effective in stopping the run.

Coach Dudley ran a play that gave teams headaches. Like DeMan's play where he ran the QB out on a pass, the Comets had a play where the QB moved from the centre when the ball was snapped, but he did not have the ball. The ball was kept between the centre's legs, and it was grabbed by the wingback, who was pretending to shuffle down the line, blocking. After moving away from the centre, the QB pretended to pitch the ball, thus forcing the defenders away from the wingback. Dudley remembers winning the southern Alberta junior high title that way with a Comet named Dallin Thompson running for a touchdown. This play was made illegal in the NCAA but can still be used in Canada.

Whatever the scheme, whether it be an odd or even front, man or zone defence, penetrating or reading defence, there is a weakness the offence can exploit. Whether the offence succeeds in exploiting the defence depends on execution and personnel. The Comets' defences were much like the Browns' in that they blitzed a lot to put additional pressure on the line of scrimmage. Teams that blitz often concede that mistakes will be made, but it is better to make aggressive ones. By putting pressure on the offence, the defence takes the initiative but sometimes makes themselves vulnerable to big plays by the offence.

BLOCKING AND TACKLING THE KEY

The last interviews I did with DeMan and Dudley were devoted to the on-field habits and schemes that the two practised. When asked what made their teams different, they both said that it was fundamentals. Their replies to the question were instant and strongly worded. They elaborated by narrowing the fundamentals to basic blocking and tackling. Both coaches were proud of their playbooks and the edge they gave their teams, but discussing blocking and tackling made them sit up straighter in their seats. When interviewed, the two gentlemen were in their eighties, and their joyful recollection of practice time allotted to skill development, conditioning, and running plays was eye opening.

Coach DeMan's mentor in the teaching of fundamentals was a coach at St. Mary's in the 1950s and 1960s named Father Whelihan. Not only did Father Whelihan coach football, boxing, track and field, basketball, and hockey, but he also was instrumental in forming the Calgary High School Athletic Association. From the beginning of the Great Depression in 1933 to the beginning of the rebellious 1960s, Father Whelihan worked with the St. Mary's staff and students. A scholarship exists in his name and states: "He taught his students the virtue of hard work and the joy of loyalty and human perfection in the ability to love others."

Tackling and blocking progressions were taught at St. Francis through live contact, blocking sleds, and bags. DeMan was especially fond of the blocking sled, which taught leg drive and teamwork. Five young men hitting the sled in unison teaches teamwork. Much like the ancient Spartans who would put their young men in a phalanx formation and tell them to move as one to topple trees, the Browns used their sled to teach players to work collectively.

Like DeMan, Dudley believed nobody should be able to block or tackle better than his Comets, regardless of his team's talent level. He devoted nearly half of the practice to fundamentals. The other half of the practice was spent working on the offence's timing. The practice was run at an unusually high tempo, and the Raymond mantra was based on the belief that fitness would be the difference-maker in the second half of each game. Jim Ralph still marvels at the superior stamina of those Dudley teams.

Dudley got to the point where he would tell his players that if they executed as they could, the opponent would be unable to stop the play even if they knew it was coming. Interestingly, former St. Francis fullback Tony Spoletini said Coach DeMan would tell his Browns precisely the same thing: "We should be able to execute the play even if they know it."

Through the dozens of interviews and conversations, there were few surprises on what made these teams great. They did not invent anything extraordinarily different but blocked, tackled, and shed blockers better than everyone. Their secret lay in their attention to detail and their drive to be champions. All of those wonderful experiences playing a tough, physical team sport helped young men who needed a blueprint for a good life.

CONCLUSION

Before the Queen's visit in 2005, Lieutenant Governor Norman Kwong was asked what he hoped Her Majesty would take away from her visit. He thought for a moment before replying. "If I can impress upon her that Alberta is doing fine and that I'm looking after her interests here and, hopefully, that we'll still prosper for many years, I think those will be my main goals."

A short time later, Kwong remarked at the unveiling of his official portrait, "I'm deeply honoured to serve the province that I love." His voice cracked, and his eyes became tearful. The province's gratitude to Kwong and his service was heartfelt. Gratitude is a beautiful virtue, and Kwong had it in abundance.

Kwong's recognition of the Eskimos' positive impact on his life spoke volumes about their effect on him. In one of his official receptions, the lieutenant governor honoured his teammates of the 1950s with a reception at Government House. Eskimos and their wives were invited and treated to the night of their lives as the lieutenant governor informed them that they had always held a special place in his heart. The game of football united men of diverse backgrounds some fifty odd years ago in ways that only they realize. The benefits of that association and those individuals are still felt today in Alberta.

The participants in the making of this book, like Kwong, believed that they were made better people through their participation in sports. The friendships made in their youth were crucial for so many reasons. It would be folly to disregard what men and women have to say about their experiences as young people and how football impacted their families, careers, and communities. All the people interviewed could quote the wisdom and values imparted by their coaches a half-century before. Quite often they had a lump in their throat, like Kwong, as they described the messages taught, the teammates lost, triumphs, and the games where they ran out of time. Football practised and played correctly brought out the best in the participants.

Brian Dudley, the founding father of southern Alberta football, talked about recently going to a game and being comforted by the sounds of young children tossing balls back and forth and chasing one another under the stands. In a few years, he knew that those youngsters would someday wear a uniform, look in the mirror, and feel the same pride their predecessors did as representatives of their families, teams, coaches, and community.

If history has taught us anything, communities and individuals must always be ready to face challenges. Today, children learn the nuances of give and take. Tomorrow, they will use those skills in their careers and with their families. Like the others, Coach Dudley used football to benefit his community by training body, mind, and spirit for perseverance, effort, resolution, balance, sacrifice, honesty, friendship, and collaboration. Football teams who score high in those areas will do the same on the scoreboard.

As adolescents seek answers to what makes a good life, so do the coaches in charge of a part of their upbringing. Before this book ends, I surrender to what others have said about what we should aim for. A more modern version of Homer arrived in the seventeenth century with the arrival of William Shakespeare. Shakespeare's characters were complicated, and he offered up a hero in one play, King Henry V, who, although flawed in his youth, matured into a man whom Shakespeare regarded as a hero.

Henry was neither the strongest nor the bravest warrior, but his courage, sensitivity, and intellect were abundant. At the battle of Agincourt in 1415, the French were first and goal on the one-yard line. Henry's men were tired and sick and wanted to return to England. The French had other plans and assembled a vastly superior force composed of the cream of the French nobility to confront the English before they could return home.

Coach Henry had a plan. His tactic for defeating the French cavalry was a "bend but do not break" defence. Henry let the French make mistakes, and they didn't disappoint. Henry chose a position that forced the French to charge across a freshly plowed field covered in mud, thus negating the horses' speed and power advantages. The French overestimated their strength and went ahead with the ill-fated charge ahead of infantry support. The French got close, but their arrogance was penalized and their forces were annihilated.

As a study of leadership, *Henry V* is an epic. Fortunately for the English and Welsh troops, Henry's leadership worked because he won the hearts of men and had the courage to lead them. Few coaches would argue with the following famous lines from *Henry V*.

In peace, there's nothing so becomes a man
As modest stillness and humility:
But when the blast of war blows in our ears,
Then imitate the action of the tiger;
Stiffen the sinews, summon up the blood,
Disguise fair nature with hard favoured rage.

I am not sure that the coaches, players, and administrators interviewed for this book read *Henry V* or the *Iliad*, but the kind of men they hoped their players would become were much like Shakespeare's young king and Homer's Odysseus. The legacy that Kadatz and Ivy left behind is still with us in Alberta. Although they are no longer physically with us, their heritage is everywhere in Alberta.

Anyone who knows the men interviewed and described in this book would find it amusing that they are on the same page as Homer and Shakespeare, and they tell similar stories.

Still, under the right circumstances, would it not be fun to see them laughing, sharing stories, and sampling the cuisine at Spolumbo's in Calgary? I'm sure these events could be organized and observed with the advent of artificial intelligence. One can only speculate, but Shakespeare would have had little experience with tomatoes and garlic and might ask for a pizza heavy on meat spiced only with salt, with mushy peas. Bob Dean from the Eskimos would have delighted in Shakespeare passing on the pepperoni pizza, as there would be more for him. Dean never met a pizza he didn't like. Forever the administrator, Dennis Kadatz would have been concerned about how the bill would be split when some ate and drank more than others. Coach Connellan would have provided much of the humour, and no one would be spared from his rapier-like cuts. Like Connellan, Kwong would have found a way to enliven the proceedings with a bet on which dish would arrive first. DeMan would have made sure that the blind Homer was taken care of and that everyone was comfortable. The city was big and confusing for Raymond's Dudley, but he would have been glad to be able to sit with Shakespeare and get ideas for future theatrical productions for his small community. Shakespeare was not familiar with musicals, and he would have taken great delight in Dudley's explanation of their effect on audiences.

The personalities of these men were diverse and unique, embodying a community spirit. The service they would receive from the staff at Spolumbo's would be as honest and sound as the work of their guests. They would not leave hungry.

Printed in Canada